About the author

Madeleine Gauché, like Darby Shaw, obviously exists, lives in Cabot Cove and does not wish to be known. She is not a ghost, because ghosts don't write. Or do they? Ghost writers do. Trying to locate her you should not; she does not desire to be found, only that the words, the lines and the lemons, are a blessing for you to pick and eat from the tree that grew from the pip that fell in the ground, died and became the lemon tree.

Love Madeleine.

LEMON TREE CONVERSATIONS

VOLUME 3

Madeleine Gauché

Lemon Tree Conversations
Volume 3

VANGUARD PAPERBACK

© Copyright 2023
Madeleine Gauché

The right of Madeleine Gauché to be identified as author of
this work has been asserted by her in accordance with the
Copyright, Designs and Patents Act 1988.

A CIP catalogue record for this title is
available from the British Library.

ISBN 978 1 80016 435 2

Vanguard Press is an imprint of
Pegasus Elliot MacKenzie Publishers Ltd.
www.pegasuspublishers.com

First Published in 2023

Vanguard Press
Sheraton House Castle Park
Cambridge England

Printed & Bound in Great Britain

Dedication

This book of poetry is dedicated to
Stephen Armstrong who "gave me eyes for eternity."

Acknowledgements

The Golden Studio for the artwork.

Contents

151
APPOINTED
NIGHT LIGHTS

Many of them in the black sky
seemingly lonely
so scattered
as if strewn from a basket
blown from a funnel

they fell, landing all over
each other, strong and weak
stuck they are, as if glued
to the ceiling, black
I stretch my neck to see-
they cover the expanse

trying I am, to understand
how they stay hanging on
in position is beyond my
comprehension, my
imagination, short-sighted my
ability limited, openly I admit

You look at me, I see, thinking
how can I talk like that
about many lonely stars
it just doesn't sit well
many and lonely

surely many cannot be lonely
thinking now I am, busy I was
going about, watching stars

lonely can mean many
ask people, they will tell
equally true is the opposite
the other end of the spectrum

but let me return
back to my lonely stars
before I lose my train of thought,
my focus zoomed
in through my lens
is perspective when

looking at the stars overcome
I become, so aware
on their behalf of the sense
of loneliness I feel so far apart
staring up into the black vastness of
space called sky
where isolated, yet bravely

they go about sparkling
trying all they can
to lessen the impact
the blackness and the dark night bring
so lonely and brave
deserving they are of medals
they have been appointed
by God

a very special task
night lights they'll be, to
come out and shine, overcome
darkness as it descends

wondering I am,
where are they when it's day,
what do they do
when the sky is blue
are they sparkling on
the other side of the world

then something moved into
position in my brain,
if that is the case
does that mean they sparkle
all the time
never lonely they are
never without their task at hand

I feel so much better now
they are always there,
it's my side of the world
that has day and night,
so glad to realise it's mine
my world is what's turning

so as time passes me by,
I will see them again
and no more lonely I will be
when my night comes
I will see them, still hanging on,
in position they sit there
all the time as they always are
have been and will be

stars are what they were
meant to be, they were
appointed divinely to be
night lights

152
WITHIN
LIMITATIONS

We talk
so aware of limitations
we have become,
the lines, the boundaries

against the backdrop of
waves crashing on rocks
so precious the
thundering background
when not there we wonder
did the breeze swing

the limitations a reality,
so aware of reality we are
now that we have moved on in age,
older we have become,
a different kind of wisdom shifted
into position

it shifted, things shift, I say,
so vivid, I can almost see

do you also believe that our Adonai works
in the background, He is
the one that re-arranges the stage,
the props, the direction of the lights,
the cue cards, the signs

remembering we'd talked about this,
in another time, about invisible signs

looking up I show you the really, really, big boat,
slowly it moves on the horizon,
its movement almost not visible on the line
where sky meets sea, equally grey,
your hair, sweet the smile
rewarding me

pictures into words and lines, is my craft,
it's what I do
to the east I look up, I see them
equally slowly, lazily they move
to the west they go, making space for blotches

blue through pink-orange
red breaks the line, the sun also slow
this morning in making its way,
the appointed day light,
reporting for duty,
time moves

day break is slow today, I say,
you equally lazy to wake
to another day of limitations real, boundaries,

I guess
the trick to find is what the limitations
allow you to do

to the east they are
now a type of silver-white beyond
my ability to describe,
I read yesterday I say,
from divine thought
to human words,

almost similarly impossible,
how the prophets got it right,
beyond my understanding it is,
to even think we are smart,
so unholy a thought to entertain

time again for me stands still,
losing myself in the sight of the eternal sky,
where is heaven, I wonder, saying to you,
speaking to friends, the sea will no more be,
is the sea the pit?

I have it now, my thoughts,
neatly in line they tow,
so relieved I am
with the result
the conversation, another one

these lemon tree conversations

fruit they render, in abundance
the river it keeps flowing,
from the tree in the middle,
salvation is to be found,
freedom from the yoke,

says Messiah,
my friend

153
THE
SOLUTION

What does one call it again, I say
into the night, quietly
not wanting yet simultaneously wanting
to wake you, to talk

you indulge my night talking
courteous and patient you are
willing to listen to me,
night talking into the far hours
of the night we walk, talking

you offer to make us
another cup
tea, we drink gallons
I see the balloons going up
into the bluest of blue skies
free, so pretty and full of colour
on delicately thin strings
down below children laugh

reminding me all of a sudden
what does one call it again?
which, you say, those
with the basket below? hot air

so special our night talks are
in the middle of the night
our talking in our midst holding promises,
the unexpected

always an element of surprise
potentially present, so precious
realising we hold on
to the glass alabaster, always
aware of our fallible hands
vividly we understand this
in the dark

careful to not let it drop
the train of thought
not quite sure even
what we're talking about
but it does not really matter

we're just awake, together
in the night, talking
it's different, don't you think
I try now to think
why it may be,
is it because in the night

sweetness is sweeter
soft softer and
gentle gentler,
quiet redefined

reminiscing now the day we met
the wonder, the discovery,
still to this day
I see your profile,
remember the gift of that
frozen moment,
kindness raining

drink, you say, it's going cold
but I'd drifted off, having said
what I wanted to, talking in the night
is what gives me so much pleasure, I see

it taking shape in the night,
balloons, blue sky, bright sun,
perspective makes its nest,
settles itself, and
when morning comes I have it

what, you say, is it you have after talking to you
in the night
the solution, I say, not realising
I had something to solve

but there is always something to solve,
there I have it now
it's what it's called
a solution
presupposing I had a problem

you just smile and we drift off
satisfied we know now
what it's called
we solved the riddle by
talking in the night
in circles which are oblong

riddles, I say, are
horses in the sea,
castles in the sky
dream houses and
lists, buckets full
we should not only live for now
there is one to come

day breaks, sheer simplicity
we have to get some sleep
wondering I am, will today
be that miraculous day,
another stone to step on
will the sign present itself
the marvel of a new dimension
added like spice, a different
flavour, a fragrance
variety to oppose monotony

I see modern day gypsies
moving their caravans
a kind of tragic sight
it stirs questions in me
how did we arrive at this point
says a friend yesterday

what did I do all these years
such a good question, you say
what is it called again
my gypsy girl,
caravans going nowhere slowly
she sings, I still hear her voice,
it echoes

can you hear it too, the echoes,
how fortunate for you
to be chosen
to hear the echoes
in the wind through your hair
soft and grey

do you have it now,
the solution? we laugh,
happy now, the purpose achieved,
chaff in the night

154
AULD
LANG SYNE

I saw that guy, I tell you
over the dinner table companionly,
congenial we are, the mood good,
always is when it's about
food has that effect,
the impact inevitably
makes us sweet
notwithstanding dessert

deserts between us disappear,
shrinks we don't need
islands pop up in the stream,
the river keeps flowing,
stones become many

to navigate the dilemma
out in the open sea, life,
realising we need a compass
safely we step on,
into our own net, lots of fish

Peter catches upon Messiah's instruction
is what we need
to guide us, so as to not strangle ourselves
catching fish
going about our daily routine,

do you love me more than these here,
three times He asks

the little flames dancing against the wall,
lazy become slow
and slow, really small
the day at the office move behind us,

we have this policy
our insurance to manage risk
we close doors on days,
at night we focus on our own affairs,
internal they're called

no ambassador needed,
intercessor not required
intermediary redundant

we pick up the morning
where we left off yesterday
we don't compromise, and
we make no allowances

serendipity, you say it's called
exactly I say,
so which guy did you see, you say,

wondering I am,
were we talking about
the guy or serendipity

are we running along
the same track,
seemingly we each are
on our own topic, clearly not
on the same page

this kind of thing happens
between us
finding each other, accidently
in the middle,
such a good discovery
stumbling upon, to this day
we laugh ourselves to pieces,

enjoying
shreds of it we see, in the wind
our candle now nearly out
no more flames
dancing against, the
shop closed, on its door astutely
the little board swings

yes, I say, this guy, he looks
a lot like you, comparatively
similar, how so, you say,
no wonder you stumbled upon,
even though no stranger you are to the night

comparatively similar
such a strange thing,
almost as inherent as relative,
the train of thought now
clearly going lost, I am
strangled in the net, only to find myself
ready to be swallowed
a Jonah I've become

forgetting was he
a prophet or priest,
or simply a disobedient messenger,
calling for
repentance in the face
of destruction,
three days then the temple will again stand,
no stone will stay untouched

time for bed, you say,
reluctance to move comes
over me, you pull me from
my chair, easy is your embrace,
as always we go up
to the higher plane

yet another, fruitful conversation
sprouting from
the dying pip,
the words become lines
the lemon tree

serendipity is what we were talking about,
comparatively similar
the guy I saw in the street,
my light will soon be out
I greet darkness, realising it's my friend
Auld Lang Syne

155
MY
ADONAI

I wonder what it was like
to walk with Messiah
for three years in tunic and sandals dusty,
not knowing the goal was the cross

I wonder what it was like when Mary washed His feet,
with oil, dried it with her hair not yet
knowing her brother would not die,
but resurrect

I wonder what it was like for
Thomas when touching
the marks on Messiah
made by the nails on the cross

You sacrificed it for us all

I wonder what it was like when Jonah,
swallowed by the fish not seeing the light,
not knowing the road without direction,
but having to go

I wonder what it was like
for the intimate circle to be told
two by two to go without rod, staff or purse,
in the world you must stay

Andrew buys the fish
let the tired people sit, twelve basketsful,
one for each
after having fed them
in groups, fifty
sufficient is grace, also for Paul,

to worship is to be obedient

I wonder what it was like
when the rich young man
confronted by the reality
having to sell all he possessed
did he realise in that moment
he was possessed?

I wonder what it was like to have been
baptized by John, repent was his message,
share your clothes, the way maker,
and then to have heard

if you can accept, he is Elijah

I wonder what it was like when
on the mountain of transfiguration,
Messiah shone, linen clothes translucent white
semi-transparent,
bright radiance,
you must not tell until

you have seen the Father because
you see me, Phillip
young John, the one He loved
In the beginning the Word was

I wonder what it was like when Cefas,
who would later be the rock, realised
he denied his Lord as it was said,
around the fire

not knowing he would three times
be forgiven to shepherd
the flock, giving he would
a powerful speech
on Pentecost, three thousand
hear their own spoken

I wonder what it was like for
the man who carried His cross
up the hill outside town
to meet
the three o'clock deadline,
surely standing by, observing
the hammering of the nails

How can I then
not call out, falling down
You are my Adonai,
in a holy impregnable domain You reign,
a little rock will come loose,
Your Kingdom, it will come,
with the clouds, every knee will bow

it is true what David said
what is the man

and yet
you measure it out for me, the
places, the inheritance in lots, the heritage
in the Pleasant Land, in green
pastures with abundant shade
growing our crops so

when I arrive I will no longer wonder
what it was like because I will be there, and
they will be too
all is forgotten, far removed
east is from west
for ten thousand years or more

How can I also not break out in joy
and adoration, the same
as the shepherds in the field,
sheep illuminated
by the army of angels,
glory to the Highest

You are also mine
my Adonai!

156
THE
YOUNG
EXECUTIVE

I saw him this morning
and something
when watching him had
my imagination captivated,
captured, vividly I see

how young is he not
but clearly cut out
an executive in the making
as they say

the saying it goes
such a laughable thing
sayings cannot go, wondering I am
where from and where to

but before I forget
lest I lose the picture in my mind's eye of
the young executive

what was about him that triggered it,
apart from the youthful look,
the suit really neat, hair styled

his walk from the shop purposeful, driven,
end in sight, oh yes,
and the tie, too sweet

sitting really well in position
thinking I am
he has his career spelt out, under control,
well in hand

master he is of his destiny
the young executive
has aspirations, I see in
how he carries himself

proudly he steps, deliberately,
to the office, believing he can
reaching for his dreams
real they can become,
at the office

where he spends his time
the young executive
in my mind now,
my imagination running
wild, no stopping

I wonder
what kind of office is it
he occupies, smart or ordinary
my guess it's really smart
by the way he looks

the young executive
funny I think to myself as he
disappears from my line of sight,
out of my circumference

how we associate, equate subconsciously,
without intent we size people up
put them in some kind of space

from what is visible to us
face value it's called
nothing I know of him I call
the young executive

I have passed judgement in spite,
labelled him, allocated him to some sort of
a sub culture, young, executive

I could not resist though in
this case, such the sight of him
took me on a goose chase
on a runway like a plane
I took off and flew

runaway, enjoying the moment
laying my eyes on this very pleasant object
a figment of my imagination of

you when you were young
and an executive, vividly you
still occupy that special space
in my mind's eye

conjuring the sweetest
memory, did he
the young executive

157
FREEDOM AND
SUBSTITUTION

It just gripped my heart yesterday,
I say to you
sitting outside the dental rooms
in the fresh air
an hour or so to spare, rare
for me to have, an hour or so
to spare, watching

people passing by, I sitting still
with my hour or so to spare,
sheer freedom I realised,
from time neither nothing other than,
nor anything else to do

just watching makes me happy
I observed of late

there are people who are free
and those who aren't
and I thought to myself watching,
so interestingly I can see
those who are free and
those who're not

and I ask myself how is it
what causes the bondage
to be absent from some,
what is it that makes them looking free?

by now I can see you cannot hold it out any longer,
what is it you see, you say,
when you see freedom and bondage

substituting your banana
an apple rather chosen,
free to substitute when
pensively reaching out

you put your hand
into the fruit bowl

I watch this,
time stands still
watching
how you pick up, put down,
and pick up, the fruit is not free
having no say in the matter,
they will be picked

chosen or not,
no free will they have,
at your mercy they are to be
substituted, you marvel in
the apple tasty,
I see it in your eyes
remarkable they are

we substitute all the time
picking up, putting down and all that
instead it contributes to us
being free or in bondage
I saw another side of this when watching yesterday

some deep thinking went on
about freedom
in substituting we exchange
not realising we do, everyone
it comes at a price,
so in the end even substitution comes at a cost,
this analysis is final

You still haven't answered me,
you say, what was that again,
I got so lost,
reliving yesterday's thoughts,
time stood still, I lost track

Freedom I realised
is the possibility to substitute,
to choose, decide
to decline or accept
priceless it is
the cost, precious enough
for us to preserve

I can see you really like that apple,
congenial the mood
substitution for the day done,
it is, said Messiah on the cross,
stepping into my place, substitutionary
so I can be free, atoned, and reconciled

Freedom I found,
in understanding
substitution

158
PASSAGES IN
THE SHIMMER

Such a thing you have never seen,
I exclaimed, waking
you open your eyes a bit,
still very sleepy, sweet you are
then wider to see what it is
that has me so captivated,
slowly you surface

and then you also see it
focusing, zooming in on
the indescribable
blue passages
made by the sun
really indescribable,

where's the camera
quick you say,
they are moving
the blue will replace the shimmer surrounds
in the realm as day breaks blue
will overtake
the shimmer
will fade away

and it's when you said it
shimmer
that I knew that was it

it was the shimmer!
the indescribable shimmer
that latched on to something
in my mind, gripped it, acutely I
realised it was extraordinary a scene, breath taking

the colour around and between
the blue passages,
a type of unending spread
gold dust, there were no rays, the entire expanse
was in shimmer and

the blue passages, almost parallel neat funnels
narrow to broad from bottom
upwards, slightly slanted
really in reality indescribable
blue passages in the shimmer

very neat, the passages
the funnels of blue, in lanes,
lines definite and precisely drawn,
a type of straight
I've never seen, did not ever
know it would be possible in the sky

such a miraculous display of order,
meticulous, clean lines
as an architect would say,
the passages in the gold dust,
shimmer completely and evenly
splashed into the sky

But is that not who He is,
the order, the plan, the lines,
putting all in its place,
all the lights, in day and night,
that is who He is, the Creator

I felt chosen
to have been revealed to
observing this special display
glory in the sky,
from where He will return,
to fetch the bride

In the beginning the Word was
it spoke creation into existence
it came, the Light,
it was the plan, all along,
intricately documented,
almost scattered,
clues here then there,

a mosaic of images conveyed
transcribed by humans,
funnels through which it flows
unmerited grace, always when I look up

I will see the very, very, neat blue passages
in the shimmer

159
FADING
DEFINITIVES

When was it

you became my friend, I ask, pondering we are,
water masses and horizons
moving further away
out of sight, mist moving in
obscuring the lines of
importance, definitives fading

pensive we are
really not ready to turn in
from spending the autumn
afternoon, watching
observing island life-
the boats, the sails, the netting,
and fishing activities- all of it
in slow motion, casting off

What is it

about island life, that
is so alluring, laid back, I think it's called,
there is no rush,
no reason for urgency,
another hour or so
makes no difference
no reason to race

all come, in good time, apparent
indifference the style, seemingly
non-committal the norm
quite acceptable,
slow-paced to which

we adapted well, considering
the short space of time, a
weekend only so long after all
is said, and done a deal
the island's become our home
so regular we frequent
after realising

we fit, befitting it's come, and
this sits well with us
lazing away the afternoon hours
the sun slowly stretching far and long,
deep into the boats
we bask in the shimmer
whisp, whisp the sails make

and all this while
I'm still trying
to find out, determine
with certainty, if possible,
the exact moment I knew
in you I have a friend

I look at you, and you just know
as we're talking in a language
not audible by those around
that kind of knowing is
beyond reason or
understanding

such the extent, the loyalty
you pledged not expressed
through words, just accepting
you will stay by my side,
come what may,

no disappointment too big,
no divide too deep,
no crossing too demanding,
no challenge insurmountable
nothing I ask is ever too much

Are you for real,
just how accommodating
can one be, when was it
the dimension settling itself
the moment I knew
you are for real, and for ever
wondering I am

do you even recognise, realise,
what this brought, just how
fruitful the acquaintance?
Never before
have I seen so much life
from a seed willing to die

We don't know
beginning from end,
time lines blur
substance, knowing it,
is what counts

When was it that we knew
being like this
is what we both want,
how it is to be
we can't really quite describe

was it in May, I say
May? you look up,
what is it about May you say
Did I say May?

not realising
I was talking out loud,
thoughts left my mind
through my lips, the gateway
my mind thoughtless,
words went
not returning

so dear you are to me,
and as we continue to talk
in our language
inaudible to those around,

the importance of definitives
keep fading away,
reality takes on a new meaning
nothing matters any more than
just us not separated by
distance or time

less and less important knowing
beginning from end, time lines become
fading definitives,
definitely we agree
and we laugh,

so enjoying this rare moment
of allowing our definitives
to fade luxuriously we gift ourselves with
fading definitives

160
NOTWITHSTANDING

We all do, walking down
the path cut out by design
as the seamstress, the pattern
neatly laid out, drawn on paper
pinned on cloth, fabric it's called

reminding me now
the fabric of life, rich in texture,
between our fingers we hold it,
as we do the glass alabaster
sometimes with complexities weaved in,
bitter and sweet
I've learned

It's a mixture, the texture
we get a bit of the one,
and the other, it's how it is
a balance of scales

the soft yellow of the lamp puts you
in the spot light you are
of my attention
in a position of serenity
through my eyes
peace surrounds you

looking up to hear me out,
lending me your ear graciously
what is it about fabric and its textures you say?
what is it that you understand?

realising again you fell
victim to my story telling
my words and I, we play
knowing though,
insight is to be gained

fabric has texture, as has life
intricately woven patterns
cut out, richly formed tracks
for us to firmly place our feet
good deeds prepared for us to walk into

to run the race, says Paul,
the eye on Christ,
the perfector of faith,
who went ahead, is the Way
we are to follow, imitate

my line of thought directed
clearly steered
venturing into the depths
of the patterns of life
exploring, running into
complexities unresolved,
realising this afresh

as we laugh about how
we are cutting the conversation to pieces,
scissors in hand
I am no seamstress after all
qualified to combine
fabric and pattern into some sort of style,

fabric cutting neatly
not always possible, our hands fallible,
neatly cut out pattern notwithstanding
So glad I am Adonai has it
neatly cut out for me

richly weaved texture
filled with patterns
clowns with baskets filled
change and choices asking for decisions
as for donations

so let me turn my attention, focus,
before pandemonium breaks out in our house,
let me keep searching,

I will find my path
what I've been cut out to do
fallible hands notwithstanding
it will be a success,

the story telling
notwithstanding

161
BEING
PRIVILEGED

Through the eyes of John who astutely
wrote the discourses, through the lens
of purpose statements,

he lends me his, the lens and
as if through a telescope
I look far far into ages past and
I see them, sitting, listening intently
as He broke the bread

I realised I am privileged
I can read and be present
in the moments John shared
when Messiah spoke to them

his inner circle, conveying
His eternal truths, the Life
the Light, opened hearts, the Way,
He did, into lives He moves

that I, in thinking it through
sharing with you- once again
you indulge me with
another cup of tea, evening approaching-
these two cardinal insights
how important perspective is,
and understanding purpose,
the aim of the discourses
joy, peace, love

that's when I think I've come to understand what
being privileged means

It does not refer to having wealth, health,
prosperity or sufficiently-provided-for needs
that to me is in completely another category,
admittedly without label currently

but being privileged now distinctly for me
has acquired a special meaning
unique the sense, being aware

I can understand
more and more
the Word is really bread,
Manna from above, sent to me so
I can feed on understanding purpose
and having perspective
joy, peace, love

I go down the path
of perspective through the
lens of purpose, deeper into
the valleys of the discourses

and as I walk gaining understanding,
the depth of the complexities
of the fabric of life
providing context,
and how to see mine, it's then

that I see exactly what
being privileged means

162
FISHERS
OF MEN

Let's talk a bit
what about, you say
oh, I don't know,
stretching out I am
eager to shed the week

just things, anything,
you can choose, I say, the topic
I will follow suit

you start busying yourself
the fire, our usual Friday night
ritual following suit
is what I Iike most to do,
especially when it comes to
your topics so surprising

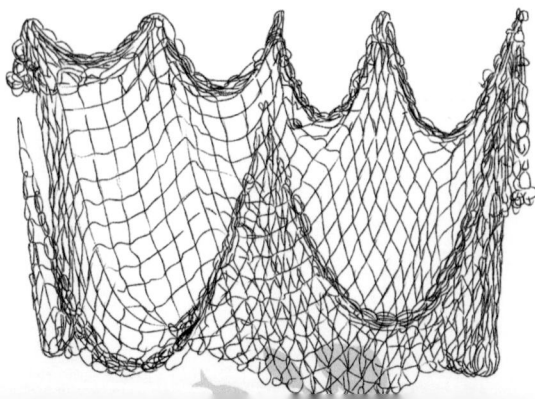

the air around us unique
in quality, surrounding us with
a stillness so soundless,
not even a single car on the tar
outside our wall
we cannot believe, so

we sit and we listen
you poured us something
to drink, and we continue
hearing nothing
as night approaches
we become one, following suit

no longer we care to choose
or to take the lead,
equal partners we've become,
willing to follow suit
in keeping, sitting, listening
into the night
our thoughts frizzling out

like the final stages of a perm,
it gets kind of funny the image
now so vivid,
we see ourselves in the salon,
hairdressers busily buzzing around dryers
making their usual noises, so familiar
together we burst out laughing

knowing time will tell the topic
will arrive, present itself,
it always does for us to follow
suit, both willing we are and
until such time,
content in waiting,
we after all don't need to talk

and
as nightfall progressively moves closer
we follow suit, two souls
one heart, united in our pursuit
to follow, closing the door on the week
in unison, resolutely

such an important attribute
outstandingly a characteristic
of Messiah's men,
don't you think, I say,
indeed, you agree

united in themselves and in Him
following suit so fundamental
a requirement above all,

Follow Me, He said,
and fishers of men you will become in
following suit

163
READING
THE OBSERVER

What again is the name, you say
looking up from where I'm busy
studying my words,
my lines, which name, I ask,
lost I am in writing

the name of the paper, you say
the one we bought that time-

that time a period
you referring to just about
as unclear to me as looking
through frosted glass-

similarly in pattern
as the paint on some
post war houses
built on plot and plan

kind of rippled
realising now
I was the observer,
wondering why the ripples
in this case in point, in the paint,
simply fascinated-

just how much did I not
love the houses in my town,
reminding me Messiah said
in the house of his Father
there'll be many places-

often as a child walking through my town
observing the houses, I recall, wondering
what will become of me
and my love of houses

So far I've now wandered off,
jolted back to reality, you stand
with a warm cup of tea
reading the observer

the waves in the background
and my reflections, I observe,
became one

you now say again,
I asked you what is the name
of the newspaper we bought
that time we travelled through
that quaint village,

oh, that time travelling
through the quaint village
now I know which is that time
you speak about
quaintness observed

and out I blurt- as it raced through my mind
like the squirrel in the gardens
after a corn it shoots
with dedicated passion
right past my feet
I had to step aside quick

walking to class when a student
right from the hostel at the top,
just below the mountain,
all the way down
through the gardens
observing
into the city, I recall now how
I use to marvel that walk

The Observer!
Yes! That's the one, you exclaimed,
you hit the nail on its head, spot on!

what a keen observer you're not,
you say, a real watchman just like Ezekiel,
watching and writing it down
a scribe such an important role
wasn't Ezra one as well, I say

just lifting your eyebrows,
slowly you move back
to your former position
reading the observer
like an open book
rather special that makes you

and whilst
busy with my words, my lines
watching I am
cut out to be an observer

writing it down that time
in the quaint village
travelling words and lines
the observer

watching you reading
the observer

164
HOOVES ON COBBLESTONE

I see the horses
round the bend stately
approaching, I hear their hooves
on cobblestone,
where I find myself, so vivid the image, I recall

cluckity cluckity cluck cluck cluck cluck cluckity
cluckity cluck cluck

for years on end if I close my eyes
I hear the sound of
hooves on cobblestone
as a train on tracks
like days gone by

there is a rhythm to it,
that peculiar sound of
hooves on cobblestone,

really many horses shiny, the
blackest of black, light foot
precisely-lifted high legs
trotting rhythmically,

cluck cluck cluck cluck cluckity cluckity cluck cluck
cluck cluck

closer and closer
the sunlight bright
the sky brilliantly blue
I completely taken up in,
absorbed by this
a moment in time

all this, lots of
parading very majestic

the riders of the black shiny horses,
regalia shining armour
red and gold, diamond white
tassles swinging obediently

under command

upright they sit
on the backs of horses
lots and lots of black,
gold and red with white
many up front and at the back

gold-gilded carriage sandwiched,
cushioned between, inside the princess
the year is 1981

on this day she became
a princess

and as I watch the scene again,
many many years
down the line I wonder
is that what being royal means
does it now make her a
daughter of the king,

realising in that moment

I am
the daughter of a King
the only one true King,
a princess I am, royal
His Majesty's glory

saying to myself
how is royalty supposed to feel
how am I to behave
when in the presence
of the king

my mind
trails off to Ester and her king
Achashverosh was his name

and it's now when
much older I am,
long gone the year 1981
again looking at that
royal wedding scene, seeing

the many black horses
the cushioned-in gold-gilded
carriage with the princess
reflecting on that exact day

understanding I
am walking in the glory
of the Majesty, royal
a princess I am
the daughter of the
only one true King and

in the many black horses I see
the Roman armies in
the many black horses

and I see a lamb
in a gold-gilded carriage
pulled, a whole parade sandwiched in,
prominence given to majestic grandeur, led

to the slaughter in
a very fast black car
the year is 1997
a princess in a parade
really, really, short lived

many black horses and
I keep seeing the Roman armies

and I have seen her come
and I have seen her go
where will she be now
killed by the Roman armies
those
many black horses'
hooves on cobblestone

cluck cluck cluck cluckity cluckity cluckity cluckity

what will become of the monarchy?

165
CIRCUMSTANCES
IDEAL

Don't you agree, I say,
jointly shared mystical shimmer
evening approaching slow
but sure, unstoppable
inevitability I am faced with
at once I feel confronted
with knowing

to get to the other side
you have to cross the Jordan
go through, be immersed

it is a fact, so certain
circumstances to be ideal
instantaneously becoming
aware of the necessity of
ideal circumstances

wanting you too to become aware,
awareness so uniquely precious,
holding the glass alabaster, hearing
in the distance
the lone guitar picked strings,

no puppets we are,
standing firmly our ground
unmovable

a feeling of sufficiency,
having in abundance,
and you smile knowingly
I am not talking
of earthly possessions,

the observer sees lots of things,
too much to tell,
but for circumstances ideal

my words and I play
my thoughts run freely
to my heart's desire,
no restrictions, no limitations
it jumbles near and far up
like a cake mix,
ingredients they become

little wagon's full
offloading its steam
at every station how quaintly you are
reading the observer, watching I

reminiscently saying,
do you recall
our conversations in the sand
castles we build in the air

we dream with our heads in the clouds

do you hear, I say, the waves
crashing on the rocks, and smilingly now,
knowing you do, words spoken
no longer necessary,
but for circumstances to be ideal

have you, I say-
realising we moved again
into circumstances ideal-

ever watched?
again trying to focus
your attention on my sayings

little children running around,
all the time laughing,
not realising their circumstances are ideal,
but for playing uninhibited
they have a pursuit

do you hear, I say,
you turn your ear too,
the breeze had swung,
salty sea air moving in
bringing the fragrance,
remembering the vanilla

cognisant I am of
my circumstances ideal,
and in that, the knowing,
realisation nestles itself,
a sweetness such as that of vanilla

and time and time again
I stand amazed,
thinking how wonderful
at this age to still be elevated
to the level of being amazed,

the tree just keeps on growing,
the pip died indeed, it fell
and it is a certainty, inevitably
it grows, but never would
I have guessed

the pip can fall in you
and the lemon tree
it grows in me

so I am awaiting May
for circumstances ideal for
you to cross the Jordan

have you ever seen such
a beautiful day break,

amazed we will arrive together
at circumstances ideal

our Adonai true to Himself moving the props,
preparing the scene, and I,
I am required
to patiently wait for, until
circumstances ideal
not run ahead of myself

and I point you in the direction of the sky
where they move, see there the observer
watching the clouds
like loose wool
they pull and stretch
like sweet little bundles sheep
creating circumstances ideal a
a brilliant blue

166
PLAYING
BELA BARTOK

I am in another realm
my own outside,
off-beat detached
from the routinely ordinary

not ordinary as if mine is special
just ordinary as in normal
the to-be-expected rhythm
the usual mundane humdrum

I stepped out from under the yoke
of boundaries,
freed myself
crossing the Jordan I find myself
on the higher plane

doing my regular
introspection I have as
my vantage point
the philosophical look out through
perspective as my lens finding
my rhythm is my own-

playing Bela Bartok
with strong hands
credited to practicing arpeggios,
I had, strong hands
the teacher said,
being ten playing the piano-
not knowing to play Bartok
strong hands are needed-

nowhere near as good though
watch and listen
the metronome
I still hear her say

walking to my piano lessons
dedication I had,
talent I believe, less,
perseverance more,
not so much the interest
but I liked going to lessons,

it was not really about playing piano
rather later I realise, but about
cross-over mental development,
mother being a teacher and all,
the left hand the right brain and all
that kind of thing

reflecting much later it can
take rather quite some time
discovering your talent
a journey requiring patience
and a nuanced approach

the balance delicate
as in playing Bela Bartok,
I played those pieces best

how does one even begin to determine to find
one's way, a mystery all along
finding the answer no guarantee
a whole life of asking, who am I

spider flowers and
dream catchers
dolphins in conversation
clowns at the door, toy trains
and stained glass planes,
minutely small pilots,

all came to me rather late,
but so sweet, these visitors,
worthwhile the wait,
I once again feel
so terribly gifted

important lessons to learn
the pursuit, the dream,
wondering often what will become-
I can, be anything
just not ordinary, if you please

rather late you and I, we met our
desires and dreams, in sync
we become one
a united front,
the space I moved into,
the shelter, hearing the metronome,
playing my own arpeggios, words, lines

I yawn, you say, should you not surrender,
exhaustion clearly visible, but I have to finish,
remember I am the one with
perseverance
leaving it incomplete
won't do justice,
to accomplish is the goal

you bring me another
fresh cup of tea,
you say it's what's needed
and I smile thanking you,
acknowledging
grateful I am, special you are

rather late but
never to find
knowing you will when you find
all along it's what you've
been looking for and it's not
playing Bela Bartok
mundane is the rhythm of the metronome,

it's rather late
the night already caressing my shoulders you say,
reconsider I should
to turn in, but how can I
the night's become the
most beautiful place,

rather late
the words and you arrived
together we are free, off beat,
not ordinary, you share
my vantage point,
rather late than never, you say,
both grateful we are,
not too much concerned about it

rather late you repeat
than never I say, join me
crossing the Jordan,
let's go to the higher plane

becoming rather late, we both hear
Bela Bartok in the
background like
crushing waves on the rocks we are

rather late in life now
we are, than never

167
AS THE
ISLANDERS DO

I wake up knowing
you are just there
down the hall in the room
just across, so close you are

the year, the turning point
or at least should I say,
the beginning of a point turning,
the tide, going out, coming in
painful, strange, very different
all I know is pressing on is what I must,
realising the importance, the significance

you visit me
for six whole long weeks
you cook, you enjoy the rugby on the television,
you rest in the soft and warm winter afternoon sun,
sleep late between the winter sheets

and I,
I bask in your presence
I am home because
I am where you are

knowing the situation is one of a kind,
one of those very rare once in a lifetime
not knowing the decline to also start soon thereafter

somehow I felt you knew
but you did not say

we share the love for the eastern winter,
nowhere else we want to be,
I so proud to show you my home,
the haven God gave me,

how much favour is too much,
grace in abundance to have given me you

I want to hold on as long as I can the moment,
in the air it is the kind of dusty fragrance
the dryish eastern winter

and suddenly I wonder what's become of my Love,
that was my name for you,
you had yours for me as well,
but that's over now, gone, done

perhaps visiting
the familiar store yesterday
is what's brought all this about

how we loved to travel,
a love cultivated from young,

so much so it became a value,
something now I must do
and regularly so to avoid withdrawal symptoms

and now
some five years down the line,
having been gifted with words and lines,
I wonder what the next five will bring,

what else
will I lose, what
will I gain, so much I already have,
the dryish eastern winter
shyly the winter sunrays move higher up
between the trees

so that by noon,
after lunch that you cooked you can rest
stretching your legs out
in the winter sun offered by
the dryish eastern winter and I

I am just happy because
we are home again
we return time and again to the
dryish eastern winter when dusty air drifts up and
into our house,
laid back we become
as the islanders do

168
IN COMPARISON

It doesn't matter
any more, how nice is that
we stepped out, sidestepping
the mainstream
off the grid, so to speak, and

we enjoy another of those
rare moments in time
laughing together,
off the grid come to think, it's
so funny, we say, we see
the same funny thing

unaffected we realise we are by
anything happening around us
it's all very short term,
the here and now
what's visible

the rest of our lives
an eternity
in comparison
eyes we have only for eternity

and yet again we know
for certain we step forward boldly

into an unknown future our protection
our armour closely fitted, like it was knitted

this perspective gives us long-term view
far beyond the here and now,
in comparison

talking like this,
conversations about comparisons,
contrasting so important
an ability to distinguish,
don't you think
to discern, decipher

chaff is different to wheat,
identifying those things
that really matter,
with what blows with the wind

in comparison
our conversation sinking down

diving into the depths
the way we like it, deep
maybe a bit too realistic,
concrete perhaps even
morbid an outlook
but we like to face reality,

look it directly in the eye,
in comparison
with beating about the bush
we don't entertain,
neither do we find it entertaining, in fact

in comparison
we find it quite appalling
to be led around by the nose,
or whatever it is called,
we after all are no circus animals

in comparison
we like the truth of the matter
we are just who we are,
simply it is the case
and we laugh,

come to think we can escape the mainstream
were we hallucinating?
again we laugh,
enjoying a moment so rare

we see the same funny thing
the guy wanting to defog our windows,
is he crazy or what,
and again we laugh hysterically
hilariously such a thought,

defogging
who would have thought
and so glad we are, we say
we see the same funny thing
we see defogged windows,
and trying to capture such a sight
in our minds

and again together
we find it funny,
a moment so rare
in comparison

169
BUYING
THE FIELD

What is it again, you say
that you told me about
last night, the young guy at office, recently married,
communication is key, I say,
he said, and we laughed for
the bluntness of this truth,
we all need the panacea,
don't we

and we at least can agree on that,
acknowledging we have to
the things of this life can be
so very alluring,
one has to tread carefully,
to avoid being taken up into
as if it is
the be all and end all

to realise real life
is not what is here and now,
it is kind of unavoidable,
don't you think, in our faces it is
every single day, but I say,
there is another way,
the Way He calls Himself,
He is the I Am
the Light and Truth

hence my need, I think,
my desire to step out
from competition, strife
all this self-advancement
and promotion, I don't want
no longer I want to participate
another race there is to run

Messiah says, who would find the treasure,
and not be very glad to have found it in the field,
and not save up all he has and buy that field

glad I am to be having
the conversation with you,
glad in fact such an understatement,
joyous closer

to the truth setting you free it will, I say,
finding it, the challenge, the journey
the pursuit to ensure you join those
grafted into the Vine

you have to find those
who journey, reach Everest,
the goal, the treasure
so you can sell all you have
in exchange for that one field,
abiding I am in Him,
loving is demonstrated by obedience,
following His command

there is a difference I say
in how we live our lives, I see,
watching you, reading the observer you say,
yes and what may that be,
offering you seem me
the panacea, you say and smile

and then it's when kindness rains into my soul,
the pip fell and the lemon tree,
grows with astonishment
I notice the abundant lemons

yes, I say, there are those
who live and lead their lives,
in the driver seat they are,
and in their peripheral vision,
somewhere just outside
the immediate circumference

they make space
for Him, no real influence
He can be and
they like it like that
as they know best

then there are those
who bought the field
having found the treasure
of putting Him in the centre,
for Him to be
the main decision maker,

the internal Guide,
the Way maker, the Word
He says surrender and
I will make smooth your path

pleasant places I will measure out for you,
store them up in heaven,
now your treasures,
find and run the real race,
pursue the one true goal,
journey to Everest where on the higher plane
lift I will, you

so you see, I say,
there is a difference in orientation

one has to find out what's it about
and buy that field, forsake, take up your cross,
lay down your life
buying the field

170
TO BE SUBTLE
CATS ARE SWEET

Never will I leave nor forsake you He said,
and I had found
it to be true, so happy I am
to have found abiding
in obedience, remaining
in love in the Vine,

the sap flows without stopping, real life,
Yochanan wrote it up so rich and multi-faceted
the discourses, the valley
for me to travel through
abundantly overflowing,
grafted in, says Paul

I disappear, become nobody
the words, the lines
take centre stage, I move back
prominence is rendered,
they feature, they come alive
they have personality
each one holds their own

this all I relay to you
stretching out you are
lazily your legs
in the dryish eastern winter sun,
the image of a cat stretching plays itself out
in my mind cats are sweet,
don't you agree, your agreement important to me,
honey is sweet too

seemingly lost
in your own thoughts too
somewhere else altogether you are
as sweet as cats
I think to myself
when up you get to serve me yet
another cup of tea
not believing you are
in saying much

and with that as in a flash,
so fast
conjuring up vividly
I'd stepped right out here, in there-

it was just a matter of time, I now realise, before
stringing words into lines
of that sweet time-

in the sun room I am
my grandparents' house,
almost all glass walls the sun room,
it used to fascinate me

I realise now,
gripping my imagination,
the glass walls, every June
get the scene, I say

cold outside bleakish but warm enough sun,
all huddled together, the whole family
grandparents too,
the cat sweet as well,

colourfully scattered
cushions so pretty,
and on top of all newspapers, magazines,
grandma's knitting baskets
and toys in the middle
we have to step over carefully

the radio playing, quiet kids father says,
grandpa has to hear the news at which
we kids just laugh
news is not important in June

tea grandma fetches and cake,
most deliciously, every June holiday afternoon,
another
picking up weight no mystery,
my mother will complain,
her skirt's waistband suddenly
cannot stretch far enough
and we kids just laugh

and after every holiday in June
we laugh repetitively about
the same sweet thing,
cats stretching out lazily
in the dryish eastern winter sun, cats
are sweet, don't you think,
June, I remind you
is holiday time

and all this time actually what's on my mind is
what I think, how does one teach someone
to be subtle

and my friend and I talk it over many cups of tea
when to apply Old Testament thought and
when not to tithe or not,
how do we discern,
God loves, I say, a glad giver

my sweet cat yet again
stretches itself out,
daintily I touch the delicate whispers,
she loves me, my cat I can see
and in the dryish eastern
winter sun I watch you
reading the observer

soon you will busy yourself
with the fire, cats are sweet
can one actually teach someone
to be subtle and should we tithe

cats are subtle, don't you think?

171
THE TEXTURE
OF LINEN

is what I feel
between my fingers,
our shop buzzing with activity,
business good,

haberdasheries strewn everywhere,
congenial the mood joyous
laughter

surrounded we are by
the texture of linen

our thing, our industry, texture
we like cloth, fabric, fibres
colours and textures we know
all we see

when we walk
down the street, happily
on a Saturday, a small respite from the week
we walk

down the street to the beach
happily the road is for
we like this particular one for
the memories it brings

where for the first time we
laid eyes on for the first time
we had sight of in a direct line
of each other for

time stood still,
a frozen moment
kindness descended and
I said I know your name

in fact, have always known,
unbeknown to you,
great your surprise,
glad and satisfied, you felt

secure, safe, immediately
I could see and I knew
you were the one
no reason for me to doubt

the possibility,
the potential ripe the hope
of the horizon, the higher plane
fruit ready for the picking

one soul from the word go
since then
many textures we felt
between our fingers together
in the distance
I hear the bagpipes
melancholy rise up in me when
past the shop they move,

I see the Scottish texture
followed by an entourage
understandably unavoidable
those sounds something else,

the shop
for those moments
come to a halt
all stand still

to hear
the pipes
and in those moments
I feel again

the texture of linen
between my fingers and see
you cutting the length
those hands I watch

your head bent,
reading the observer
through your soft grey hair
your beautiful eyes focused

the customer in waiting
attention diverted by the pipes
the band in Scottish texture
and I recall how we used to like

walking down the street
to the beach
a happy road for us, down
and between my fingers I feel

the texture of linen

and I can't help but thinking
about the Man in the middle
in linen, feet either side
of the river, telling Daniel, write

flowing freely from the middle and
I see the tree with the fruit
ready for the picking
lemon after lemon
conversations I continue
having even long after
you'd gone hearing the pipes

lost I am in thought
I stand in our shop now
melancholy rising up in me
seeing again
you cutting the length

while through the window
I see the Scottish band
their entourage in tow
feeling between my fingers

the texture of linen

and

kindness descends
becoming part
of the texture
clothing myself I am in linen

172
ON THE
RADIO

is where I heard it, I say to you
the story about
while watching
deep into the blue of the sea
the air around
the quietest quiet
you cannot imagine how

I just see blue
in the sea, blue
in the sky, here and there
specs of loose wool white,
and on the land lots
of green and it's quiet
the way we like it

so in any case, I say,
on the radio it was,
the story broke

realising just how much happened
in just one year, feeling like a millennium
so much so the impact of the happenings
wondering then now I am

how will the next one be
basking in the soft dry eastern winter sun
you sit, legs stretched out,
the cat also content, kindness descended

and what I hear is the end of
the church dispensation,
when I heard
all the more churches are becoming empty
the shofar sounded, the trumpet

and wondering I am
how many more should blow,
John wrote while on Patmos
in the Spirit on the Lord's day

Just think how far
into the future he was shown
to see, when in comparison I
can only see the line of the horizon,
where sea meets sky

when Christ reveals
He shows a lot
far into the future

judgement on its way
repent John said,
not John of Patmos,
just so you don't get confused

and stumble, says Messiah,
love one another and abide,
keep my command,
bear fruit else you will be cut from the Vine

realising I went completely
off track, you waiting
for the story that broke
on the radio,

but you don't mind
me going off track,
it's the usual story,
the radio being completely forgotten,
story lost, but for

about the church dispensation
the era of grace,
I want to talk to you about
the menorah being removed,
first love forsaken
time is running out,
He stands by the door, knocking

while Messiah said trust in Me
never forsake will I you,
but they could not even stay awake
for a wee bit of time, weak flesh due

the sky now a type of blue, brilliant I think
as on the day of the funeral of the princess,
the monarchy under threat,

a Kingdom to be restored,
Messiah to reign,
the fourth temple,
a thousand years,
amazing is the grace,

when beyond the Yarden it sits,
the beautiful land, promised
pleasant the places measured out
but nations to be eliminated,
idols turned away from,
Adonai fights the battle though

you try again
to ascertain
what was the story
that broke
on the radio
a futile attempt we laugh at,

the wind out the sails
momentum completely gone,
blowing the story
in another direction,
the breeze must have swung

caught up as fish in the nets-
they huddle, throw out on the other side,
enough to feed thousands-

are the words and the lines
another conversation
going its own way, it does
and it does not matter for

on the radio
another story
will break

173
PATIENCE
IS A VIRTUE

Whirlwind tours people call it
when it goes fast on the move
from the one to the other,
station to station, city to city

in and out
those yellow cabs
moving like ants,
just busier

reminding me now of our rush
to get to the ballet in time
sweet the times were

in the distance I hear
church bells ringing
small village life
where I feel at home
slow the pace, we have time

appreciating the sun
rising and setting
walking to the market
basket in hand
fresh produce for the weekend
and cake as well to go
with afternoon tea

whirlwind tours a thing of the past
when we still performed
on stages we spent our lives
in dressing rooms,
press conferences, dinners

so glad to have been able to
stepping out, no more madness
we now enjoy living
the slow life, time we have

watching the boats
in the harbour, whisp whisp
the sails make, cafe lights coming on and
you busy yourself with the fire

thinking I am, what lovely hands you have,
I cannot get enough,
never I tire of watching them,
willing you are Friday night after Friday night
to make the fire,
magic flames dancing against the wall

waiting for me to start
my stories, inevitably
I'll have a fresh one,

that you know, is as certain
as summer is warm

and I hear you laughing
by yourself

sure I am you are recalling the moment
me telling you the story about snowmen in summer
that night behind the tree I see
in our garden

the plot for this evening
brewing, as the coffee
in the pot,
new beans you bought
for us to try, espresso
sensually the fragrance blends
with the smoke of the fire

so easily we are
making the transition,
switching from whirl winding
on the stage to weekending
in the village from dusk to night

and all the time in the world
we have to listen
to our hearts beating as one, in sync

maybe my story telling
will follow in the night, who knows,
the stories come at random, unannounced,
without forewarning they visit
at the strangest of times,

not dictated to they are,
each a personality of their own,
firm they stand their ground,
quite astute and resolute,

I tell you and we laugh
they just arrive
at the doorstep like the clown with baskets full
changes and choices
asking for decisions as if for donations

and until that time
we wait because
patience is a virtue,
realising though,

we did hear
the story for tonight,

on the radio it broke, sensational,
we agree in unison, let's turn in
then perhaps in time

sooner than later they will arrive
and we will be there ready
to welcome them in because

patience is a virtue,
benefit for the reaping

174
THE
PHOTOGRAPHER

I want to tell you
something, I say, ah yes, you say
not minding me waking you,
seemingly the story had arrived,
better, you realise, to get ready
for the conversation

in the middle of the night black,
the ocean's roar
a constant companion
through our windows,
natural as pretty close to the waves we are,

so loud-
I guess if you come from a farm,
where quiet nights rule, this roaring will take
some time getting used to-

I want to tell you I saw today
the funniest thing,
so glad I am
I can still see the

funny side of things having
sides is what's so funny

you not sure you follow,
given it being in the middle
of the night and all of that

but having learnt benefit is
for the reaping from patience, so
you persevere

yes, I say, it was like this
completely taken by surprise
by the funny side of things,
conjuring in my mind, this guy
I see with the camera

bending and stretching
in all sorts of directions
zooming in and out,
looking like a gymnast
busy with floor exercises,
but really slow in motion,
quite artistic, acrobatic

in a sense almost cat-like
depending on how you look at it
your angle of things
prescribing which side of things you will see

he bent and he stretched
his body into the funniest
positions you can imagine,
and I

I was so mesmerized,
I stopped to look, staring
more accurate a description,
until he became aware of me and waved

then I thought by myself
just who is this guy
zooming in and out,
possibly a fancy magazine photographer
photographing our modest wild coast waves

and all of a sudden all of
it became so funny, I see
the funny side of things
he must have seen given all
the bending and stretching,

so much so he brought me
to a standstill, captured I am,
I realised, completely captivated by island life
I noticed through his lens, noticing

you drifted off, it has this effect,
my conversations
about seeing the funny side
of things and I laugh too
thinking of the angles that guy took,

what do I know he took
behind my back as happily I finally started
walking again, home

so blessed I realise anew
with a young spirit,
I can laugh,
I still find things funny
and I see the funny side
of things, let us, I say to you,
not take ourselves too seriously,

but if you heard or not I
don't know drifting off,
the photographer bending and stretching,
zooming still making me laugh and will, I think
for time to come, since
that's how I deal
with the tragedies of life

175
YOU CAN
TALK TO ME ABOUT

My young spirit
has caused me agony,
believe it or not,
being the same age as those
born in your year,
so everything should be the same,
all things being equal,
but don't you believe

as I had received a young spirit,
it does not age, or at least, I should say,
it's aging much slower than those
born in my year

and looking back at many awkward moments,
I came to understand
at the root of it all was the young spirit,
it's the best way I can call it,
this that's living inside me-

slow I was in emotional development,
envying those around me, being so mature,
not realising life is a long affair,
and we need lots of joy
carrying us through,
and I smiled to myself,

mischievous my friends called me,
so funny, asking
what are the secrets
I carry around

now knowing at age sixty,
I was observing,
a lifetime of images
I was storing
in my photographic memory-

it's quite a strange thing
always being a bit out of sync
with your peers, and for long it bothered me,
since I could not give it a name,
did not know how I should deal with it

until one day in the Golden Gate,
I'd already reached
the age of fifty-five,
and was fuelling up when
it dawned on me,
shot in like an arrow
and I knew that was the gift,

super strange gift, I remember saying to God,
Yet simultaneously acknowledging,
God does not make errors

I realised in my old age to come
when my body perhaps can no longer keep up,
it will be my young spirit
that will be sustaining me,
and obviously for a big portion of my life,
most of it, out of sync with my peers,
have I been and will I be

so I say you can talk to me about
being out of sync, I know how it feels,
being out of sync

I recognised in you a spirit
matching mine,
do you even realise how rare
an occurrence that is,
the matching spirits

that is why our parting
made me so sad,
engulfing me in sadness,
but fortunately my young spirit is
what's pulling me through
and I've grown up a bit

knowing not to concern myself with
being out of sync, understanding it is
I who have the advantage,
being a bit disassociated,
some days not so easy,

but

then to remind myself just how unique this gift is,
and again I feel chosen,

now you

just have to cross the Yarden,
into the promised land, to claim
your place measured out
for you
and I

I have to be patient and wait
for God's timing,
nothing in life is futile,
borrow my lens,
adjust your angle

and see how funny is the photographer,
snapping pictures cat-like in stretching,
zooming in and out
getting a different perspective

on being out of sync
you can talk to me about

176
MINDFUL
OF HOLES

You are so dear
you see as I stepped into
the house, I have turmoil
to process

How do I even describe the
emotions running all over the place
inside my heart and mind
needing to understand,

I have more questions
than answers, wrestling I am,
then I'm on top
then the questions
the answers have not yet surfaced,
in the rink

where do I begin to create order,
distinguish, classify and sort
which bundle to go where
what do I do when being bombarded by
so many things versatile in nature
a complete understatement

Time you'll give me,
that you know for starters is
what'll work for me
to start the process of sifting

the problem is the sifting
my mind is full of holes,
it feels like all are falling through

I am almost sure a bombarded brain
must reflect some kind of signs,
biologically I mean
it has to be, but nevertheless
the turmoil has to be dealt with

neatly I have to file each piece away,
labelled and organised
it has to become,

this running around like kindergarten children
all over my heart and mind
as if over a playground
will have to be stopped
dead in its tracks

where do I even begin
the questions are all over the show,
stealing the limelight
and I am at a loss,

getting it right to smile,
only a little though
why don't you begin,
one story at a time, you say
and I resolve,
perhaps that is a good idea

accept is the secret
to let it go, coming to grips with to know and
quickly to switch from to
reminding myself all things work together for good

and I'm
not buying into a sentimental interpretation of the text

but immediately I am to accept
if things don't go as planned
or as you'd been requested,
re-orientation is critical, I see
forgiveness is key, freedom
complete and ultimately

to calm down the sea,
the turmoil in waves crashing over my head
God has a plan, I have to know
my job is to give Him the space,
to redirect as He wants
to do another thing, get me
to take another turn

unknown at that point in time
totally unseen
beyond comprehension,
but stop He must me
so to follow suit and
do as He says is what's needed

bearing in mind
He does not talk in a human voice,
but talk He does,
His guidance His voice
so to develop the sense to detect the guidance
is what's the trick

I feel so much better now having spilt the beans
patiently you absorbed all and
for that I love you all the more

you can take it all and more,
you say, together we
will work our way through
the questions
towards the answers, and
a mind that can hold it all
nicely together,
labelled and organised

177
SHE CALLS
ME FLOWER

I saw her today at the store,
I tell you, as we find ourselves awake
in the dark night
watching

the yellowest of yellow moon,
exactly half of full, really big
and that's quite fat
balancing itself
on the round side,

complete as if cut from cheese
mature-

so funny to refer to the moon
as mature cheese
but as funny as it may sound,
it's astoundingly so
the night otherwise pitch dark-

and as we watch we see
the moon move father east,
completely horizontally it glides as if pulled along
on a sleigh, gently
it is master of the sky

it looks like it's rising, I say
to think, a rising moon
what is the effect on the tide,
I wonder, knowledge of tides
not my strong point

who is it you saw, you say
oh yes, where was I

it's that hairdresser, that tall one
with the warmest lovely brown hair
and brown eyes,
who has the salon on the corner

calling me flower
every time when she sees me
anywhere in the street
she says
hello flower,

and every time I naturally smile,
ice broken immediately defences down
so sweet to be called flower,

when she says it like that
I feel grace bestowed
a beam of radiance
shines in my direction

every time when
she says hello flower

the way in which she says it
is what is remarkably unique,
breaking through any wall
I may think I had erected
around to protect me,
unpretentious is what she is,
it struck me anew

the moon now decidedly moving east,
higher up, ever so slightly tilted,
and less yellow, more pearly,
still fat, the ocean still roaring quite audible

while I keep hearing her voice
calling me flower,

that is the thing about my village
and the life I'm able to live,
meeting the hairdresser,
popping into the butcher,
everything one minute away,
small and close,

I'm not made for the city,
I realise afresh,

the lack of genuineness,
the rush, the noise relentless in its pursuit,
the cars, people in and out malls

no chance of meeting the hairdresser
of the salon on the corner,
calling me flower

178
RUNNING A
COMMENTARY

I find that
quite often,
I land myself at a point
don't you also,
most people do,
more often than not

sometimes one of no return,
and then other times
the point is not clear,
but a point nevertheless
direction becomes fuzzy,

irrevocably I find
the turn of events sometimes
around a corner, I laugh
and you know
I saw another funny thing,

a man trying his best to come
around the corner
against the wind, his coat
plastered against him,
umbrella flipping-like,
completely uncontrollably
I go on laughing,

satirical you say, I am
you have not heard everything,
I said, I told
a colleague yesterday

let's kill many cats with one slap
and even
in the midst of the conversation,
seriousness gone,
he could not contain
his laughter just bubbled up

saying he's heard about killing
many birds with one stone
but not the cat version and realise I did,

admitting
running a commentary is what I do,
it's everywhere,
my sight of things
just all over the place
and make no mistake, no oversight it is,
nothing goes missed

When asked what is it that you write about,
all the words and lines, acknowledging
running a commentary, I do

Looking east I see
every day break with its own colours
it puts on display,
not one is the same and I
think about chiasms and parallelisms

and the Word that became flesh
to live among us, only begotten,
the First fruits from the dead,
look John, says Messiah, write
I was dead and now I am alive,

include all the communities,
all seven of them,
they must heed Me
to live eternally

there you did it again, you said,
running a commentary,
running along I am,
my words and lines
having a will of its own,
a point of no return

and no relay race this is,
handing batons over
in pairs of four,
I was always number four,
being fastest and all of that shortest as well,
but boy could I run!

the sky now turned bleak
or is it grey, overcast
with no clear line of division
to show where the ocean starts,
it's all one large display of grey,
coolish too the sea air
salty rising up on the balcony
finding its way into my room

and yesterday I saw
just as the bread and fish
left Messiah's hands, in pieces
many baskets full,
until all were fed,
even with twelve baskets left,

my words and lines stream from my fingers,
never ending,
that was the promise,
streams of living water

and I

see what this looks like in reality,
just how blessed
can one be this side of the grave
I have said this before, privileged

Go run you race
a commentary to deliver,
conquer, pick up your cross,
lay down your life,
do we even know
what that looks like,
dying to yourself

We have absolutely no idea
It's all about us, we will
have to renew our minds
is today's commentary
let me run

enough is enough,
the point of return
draw the line
be born again

You are a rabbi and you don't know!

179
TIME ON
MY HANDS

is the gift
I hold it,
in my fallible hands
time runs
through the hour glass,
the sand many minute little
granules so fine,

uncountable
they just flow through,
running very fast in minutes
it ticks its way and onwards
it marches, unstoppable

and I can choose
what a privilege to be able to
exercise choice,
so much freedom I see
in choosing how
to spend my time

spending time
such a strange phenomenon
just think
money something to be spent
time is to be held on to-
a moment may not come around again

I see the choices people make
they keep on filling time, but I

I choose to not fill time
I like to sit moving along
or rather should I say
being moved
with and by time,
allowing it to provide my pace-

I can adjust the metronome to suit my pace
tick tick
tick tick it makes
sitting on the piano, proud-

experiencing moments
being aware of the atmosphere
you can only become if you
simply sit and you just are

contemplating, reflecting
hearing
the birds, the sea
smelling
the salty sea air
seeing
the blue of the sky, vastness
and the white of the clouds

thinking I am
I can
forgive anybody any and every thing
if just I
can sit like this in time and
in time all will be all right

marvelling I am in the simplest
of things, watching I am
the changing colours in the sky
indescribable, the clouds
so soft, I see
and it's like I touch it
with my hands, bundles of it

thinking again I am with fondness
whilst laughing by myself
I was looking through the lens
yesterday, seeing them all
outsmarting they are,
no holding them back

so you see
that is why I like to choose how
I will work with my time,
I get to learn wonderful things
that otherwise would pass me by,

how poor will I
not become without
time on my hands

180
THE
LAST HOUR

of the day is my favourite, so
it was just a matter of time
for words and lines
about this to flow from my fingers

following the others

into the last hour of the day
one moves rapidly through the working day,
looking forward to the last hour of the day
before sunset, special

we grew up like that
with that idea
the last hour of the day
before sunset to be special,
treasured

mom and dad
outside on the patio
catching up, content
what a privilege
such pretty picture
I find in them

touching base
with each other,
us kids giving them space
I to keep the twins occupied under control,
until big sister arrives

the rascals
a double dose of energy
they are, the little dynamites,
red curls like carrots,
mischief written all over
the faces naughty, always
up to something up the sleeve,
right up their ally

and I get lost in thought,
the rascals colouring in,
mom and dad catching up,
I watching

colours becoming defined by lines confining

thinking about another last hour,
John wrote,

little children it is
the last hour, in the last days
God spoke through his Son
the time of the prophets done
it's over, period concluded,
and Messiah on the cross
it is finished He says

mission accomplished,
I will not lose one of them
You gave me
out of my hands nobody will snatch them,

and so
the church dispensation will also
run its course,
sand flows through the hour glass

so safe I feel
knowing neither fire
nor river can harm me
that was the promise and
on His Word I take Him

and suddenly back to reality
big sister's arrival the sign for
rascals to run, pandemonium,
lots of joy, peace on the patio
a thing of the past, the last

hour of
the day
over it is,
mom calls dinner is ready
all six of us, around the table
dad says grace,
how grateful we are for sharing
the last hour

181
I SEE
WHAT YOU SAY

Have you noticed, I say to you-

glad
for again we have a moment together
to just talk-

how often people say
I see what you say

and when I hear people say
I see what you say, I wonder what is
meant
when they say
I see what you say

because words cannot be seen
or can they, do we see pictures
when we hear words
or is it just a form of expression

when walking down
the familiar road seeing people
saying lots of things
while walking down the familiar road

to the beach and seeing I am you thinking,
trying to see what I say

and guessing I am it is
another illustration, a form of expression, us making
pictures of words

and unavoidably I go
down the familiar road
my mind travels back again and again
to all the men being shown pictures
having to turn them into words
for it to be written down,

look John, Daniel, and write it down,
and Ezekiel and Jeremiah acting it out,
so people could see

in the many long ages
before Messiah descended from heaven to become a
Man-
Son of, many of them called Him-

they all saw the same thing
right through the ages up to John,

take that as confirmed,
revealed Messiah incarnate,
Word became flesh so they could see
what is being said, John said they,
his followers at that time touched Him,
a new command

and I
I stand amazed
where there is no light, it is dark
such a simple thing, but profoundly the truth
it struck me afresh my senses
acutely aware I am

and I see what a life looks where His light
is not shining, it spirals down
into the depths of darkness,
a pit called depression
in modern times, that's the problem, I think and see

times have become modern

and all this time while walking down
the familiar road I see you seeing what I'm saying

seeing today through the lens of the ages,
to interpret,

and asking Him, I am
to show me, to interpret
and translate for me
to understand against the background,
on the stage of modern times, the context of
of currency

which of the pictures He showed John in particular,
are playing themselves out right
in front of my eyes, please let me see,
I ask, give me the light
so that I don't walk in darkness

and you
you say, almost not audible
so soft
I see what you say

and we continue
walking down
the road to the beach
overly familiar it is,
we say and we see

182
IN ABEYANCE
IN MAY

you and I, we hang around,
lounging, loosely basking
each in the other's closeness
where many words
not necessary to say much
not required, and
we continue drifting

it's just enough for us to be,
drifting we sustain ourselves
we agree, wholeheartedly,
totally in totality we are
in agreement, wholly critical
to be

one mind to be one soul,
two by one and we laugh lazily,
entirely it's just the way we see
we like it to be, wrapped up
shielding each in the other's softness,
protection

at bay, in abeyance we keep
what will disturb the peace,
it's just our way, how we pick pieces
and patterns we make
in the May sky,
we play and
we make fun, we make,
the shadows big then none

we don't like things off-centre
equilibriums we keep at bay
and looking over the bay,
our much loved, we realise

it's just

for us the place to be
over the bay in the May sky all is slow
and lazy and we float around in the sky,
in May, keeping at bay what will throw off
balance
the equilibrium

at arm's length we keep in abeyance,
closely we hang low through the early hours
almost touching the edge of the ocean
knowing as night becomes day
higher up we will float
out the way,

keeping us
at bay it's just that
day will overtake us
quite rightly so,

the throne now belonging
to the sky entirely in its entirety blue,
vastness the majority,
it has taken over, it reigns,
its turn to keep us at bay,
in abeyance we will be kept
at arm's length

and that is order with us,
we understand, each having their roles to play
in the sky
in abeyance in May

from far
as night comes closer we
again move to the line so thin
between sea and sky,
horizon we think, is what it's called by humans
when they talk

and we gather around,
we become the border, drifting
back into our position
lining the horizon
over the bay
in the sky in abeyance
in May
we keep the day

183
THE
ACTORS

I notice them everywhere
the actors, as if on a stage
they are, displaying they are

their strength and authority
life, they have it covered
importantly they rise

in their own estimation
formerly normal they were
now somebody to reckon with

to consider, a domain they now have,
a territory to be master of
rising up, a star to watch

like never before,
shooting up with speed,
no doubt they endeavour to convince

us the audience

fading into the background
playing minor roles, if any at all,
as we watch this

I, me, and myself,
deserving, having climbed the ladder,
right on the top now

retreating, no wish I have
to participate in the act,
thinking I am, no desire I have

to compete for centre stage
the limelight never has been
for me the prize to win

and continuing my line of thought,
in my silence, observing the actors around me

I wonder when her highness
will come to a fall,
even Babylon fell
is it just a matter of time,

I stand amazed,
this actor unrecognisable to me,
my former friend, what has become

of being humble and
disgusted I become,
so terribly disgusting I'm
starting to find this, the acting,
just wanting to not have any part in this play,

trying I am to find a way
to end this, the pretence,
no star you are in my eyes,

in fact, quite the opposite
I see how the world got hold of you
and as I leave the scene,

I wonder
how long will
this facade last

because our Father God
does not tolerate this highness in own eyes,
smart and clever,

it comes just before the fall,
some have their reward in this life, I think,
departing, leaving

the actors

behind while they are still
having fun, self-importance
still in the driving seat,

and I cringe for when not
do they drive themselves
into a tree,

pieces of self
flying around like sources,
for others to pick up,

and from psalms I learn,
I see the end and content I arrive home,
knowing

joy is not found in the things of this world,
passing in nature they are, the alluring quality

short in comparison,
nothing in reality, life on the stage,
short the acting career

like chaff
in the wind, these acting
opportunities are for

the actors,
and leave them
be, I will
knowing I found the field

184
THE
SCRIPT

It's in the script, I say
our lines for the next day
we have to learn them
the lines, the script has them
prescribed for us to narrate
playing it out loud, our roles

from one episode to the next
up front they are,
spelt out in advance for us
to follow our lines,
no deviations allowed from the script
from nowhere to the plot

there always is a plot
the pinnacle of the drama,
having to build it up we narrate the lines
towards the intricacies,

delicately
I catch myself, my own way I go,
lost, in the background
the lines become less important
I write my own script,
my own words and lines,

life in abundance is a reality,
as is the Day of the Lord and the
coming of the Messiah
to resurrect the church,
and with it the Spirit also returns,

back to the unity in the trinity,
Three-in-One, and united gentile and jew will be,
says Paul to the community,
the ones who lost their first love

fallen away, apostasy,
no turning back, be careful to not to
is the warning that goes out to the fallen world,

heed the warning,
the unknown writer says to the Hebrews,
there is a great cloud
witnesses to spur you on,
run the race to win the prize,
reach the finishing line,
the end of the script

and yawning, I say, this is it,
I've reached the end of my line,
fatigued I close
the script to
the end of my day

I move away, into sleep land I will go,
reconciling, making friends with
my purpose, catching up and align,
understanding the lines of
my script,

drifting off, into the background I go,
collecting my material to the forefront of my mind
they come, the new lines
stringed along by words
towing the line,
each of them having a place in
my script

and happy I am
I am writing my own
words and lines and in such good company they are,

they become
our script

185
MAPPED
OUT

We sit, fascinated
by the map
having studied

the rise of Europe to include
the Americas and Australia,
colonising the world,
the reach of the Roman Empire

astounding in stature and
force majeure, Latin every-
where
hellenistically it marched

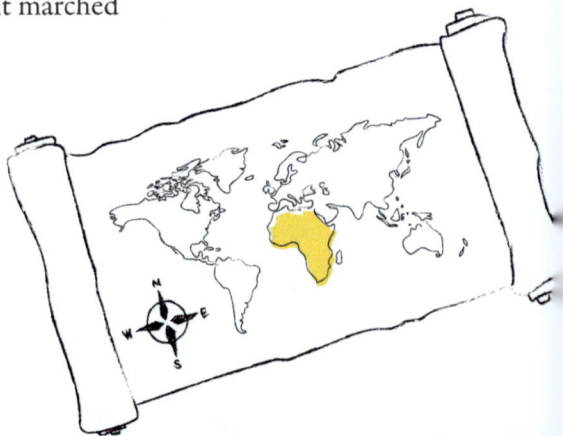

overwhelming them
conquering, trampling their
land no longer under their
reign, governance not their own

right into the times of the nations
they marched into the ages to come,
the nations

It's all there mapped out in the Word,
puzzle pieces to be put together,
here then there, I think, I say,
I have said this before,

astonished afresh I am by
the course of events, mapped out,
well in advance, time is ticking

the main event imminent, the
moment, opening the scroll
breaking the seals
in succession they will go,

the horses will run,
introducing they will,
Jacob's trouble

the final seven
years of great distress
discipline to save
the remnant

all Isra-El will be saved
mapped out in history
it is, influences,
and I see periods, the movement

the great I AM

realising I am on holy ground
in awe I stand, minute I am
no stature I have

just glad I could be considered
worthy enough, chosen to
receive righteousness
and continuing we are

reading the Map
not in a straight line,
nevertheless we continue
knowing all we see,

in time
it's mapped out
and I point out to you

the eastern sky, where again
the display
just takes our breath away,
privileged we feel to see,

to those who knock,
the door will be opened,
if you seek you will find and
the Seed will grow

in my Father's house
there are many places,
and when it's ready, I will come for you,
the bride to be

the Kingdom, the rule,
the Only One, Messiah
is His Name, it's all there

mapped out
in time, times and half a time

186
IN SOLITUDE

and isolation
Messiah said in being still
He will meet you
to lead you to quiet waters He wants

you to drink
from the fountain
of living waters,
eat from the bread
of life,
never to thirst or go hungry

He said for Him to live
it's necessary to do His Father's will
and in solitude He went,
regularly seeking His Father's face

shouldn't we then learn
from this example to go into solitude
it's where we will find the answers,

first and foremost, though
dealing with the questions,
interpretation such an important thing
to get to the bottom of
our own understanding

in solitude to confine yourself
to the space in seeking Messiah's face,
quietly on your own
and He will reveal all there is
to know to equip you to deal
with all you are confronted with

no other way there is,
I found, only the Way,
in there is life and light to be found,
all seeking put to the end
when still you become

in solitude you will find
what you have been seeking for
trust me, I say, truthfully you can obey
and follow the example
going into solitude

you will be rewarded, and find
what you have been looking for
 no more seeking,
to an end it's come,
brought about by solitude

187
SURROUNDED
BY GLASS

There always is, I say to you,
an explanation, I've learnt
you just have to find it

This I say to you after having heard
you telling me the story you heard
from our neighbour you met at the store,

such an interesting story
he told you, you say and wondering
why this may be the case,
no seemingly explanation, you say,
the neighbour said,
for what he encountered

sitting we are in the winter sun,
rays full of brightness falling in abundance

into our sunroom
surrounded by glass
allowing all of what's outside
to be part of what's inside

having once again
one of those really lazy days, special and rare
a Saturday
on the eastern coast in May,
making the most of the sun
in our room surrounded by glass

a special month for us,
seemingly we use it for reflection, evaluation
and consideration, lots of comparisons too

since we reached a stage
we realised,
we really like to be together,
no rough edges to us
being with each other,
no longer we need many words

complete we have become
one of mind and intention
zoomed in, the focus the same
purpose not split and it's then when I say,
there always is

an explanation, it's there,
it just has to be found,
to be reasoned out

the reality, however, is
explanations come to you
in different forms, shapes and sizes,
nature often obscured

so not apparent the connection
the link not immediate, what
you were wondering about,
the explanation, and

I see you listening
all ears you are and I
I feel encouraged to continue

you have to be on the lookout,
listen with discernment
explanations are like that,

you sometimes cannot quite catch,
capture and understand,
but if you give it time, it will

crystallise itself out,
sufficiently it will give you the words
equipping your mind to understand It was

the explanation
as explanations go,
they will present themselves
to you, an open mind
is what you need to determine,

recognise it when comes to mind,
very softly knocking sometimes,
no, mostly actually

because in words they come,
fertile ground you need,
to water it regularly, creating

sufficient circumference
surrounded by glass,
then you will see
the limitless sky
how far a horizon can be

if surrounded by glass
the explanation will be seen
with the eyes of the heart
clear as crystal
through the glass

188
OCEAN
LANGUAGE

I am
leaving the battle field for the soldiers

no desire to fight
no longer interested I am
all this dancing around, defending my cause,
frivolous I judge it to be

standing back, I am,
rest assured, leaving
the battlefield to the soldiers, letting them

enjoying the battle seemingly
is what I see
on the field they battle
the way forward,

and I also see
you know to leave me until my story reached its end,
marching in the parade no longer my desire,

knowing the solution,
the way forward will present itself very soon,
standing back
you will

suddenly comically the situation
has become
my desperation to be
understood and heard
trying so hard, and

you say
calm down,
your message is received,
loud and clear
speeches being delivered
you quite used to by now

and I forget who you are,
no enemy
my fellow dolphin
my partner in the ballet,
looking up to the girl with the strings,
tilting I am to you my light blue checkered hat
in the shimmer, the dusk,
the waves,
how do I even begin to describe
that hushing roaring unique,

ocean language,
I think I will call it
Have you heard it, I say, the
ocean language,
you have to stay a bit,
hang around the ocean,
to hear the waves speak
ocean language,

and I cannot think of something
more breath-taking,
just near the waves I want to be

so shall we, I say,
let's dive right in partner,
next wave is yours,
and we play
our wave riding games,

soldiers on the battlefield
long gone from memory
washed away
by the waves in the ocean

every time we emerge from
under the waves, the world
looks washed, realising it is
us, washed we are, baptised
forgiven, we were dead,
now alive we are

and suddenly I understood
what living in the waves is like,
I hear them talk

and accepted I feel
understanding the language of
the ocean, a dolphin I became

now too I can,
to live in the waves
I had to become
a dolphin and in unison—
quite a pair we are—
we dive in again, one-of-a-kind listening
to ocean language
Happiness is such a rare thing

189
GIVEN

I hear over the radio
the gift of the givers
intervened, the severity
the situation dire

it is a given, I say
giving you the look that only you know to
understand you do so
through love, leaving me
given the situation
having given me

another cup of tea
in hand you stand

gifted I feel I am, having received you
to ensure the gift can keep flowing through,
the little fish and small
pieces of bread broken

manna like snowflakes,
both come from above, Messiah too

and against the glass of the window
I trace with my fingers the lines
the raindrops running down make
and I think of the given that life brings,
lots of givens

and given situations are
what direct our path,
not always realising
how subtle they are,
but a major role player,
a co-actor when all we thought, we are
alone
given
the situation

but don't be a fool or fooled, things are never
what they look like, apparent to
the human eye,
given the complexity
far beyond visible to the eye

given to see
only what is on display

ever so slight your movement
delicate the balance,
in the scales, but observable I see you do follow
my monologuing on and on

this too is a given and that makes you loved

given the circumstances I said let's do it,
let's learn a language a special,
our own, suited to us, given I have been living
with the given, so long,
happy I am with it by now

you on the other hand,
I see, struggle, not with speech,
but the fact of the given,
wanting perhaps it not to be,

yet

acceptance I believe,
is a gift, opportunity for adjustment
providing a given,
the only requirement,
you should see in that light
requiring you to change your lens,
I say, again

you can do so much given
being loved,
fulfilled you can be
given acceptance for the beauty inside I see,
and the words you speak
those beautiful eyes, I read

being a really good reader,
I am ahearer too, especially
of the unspoken
quite funny given,

but then I remembered
I hear with my heart, I see too
you need to let go,
so you can be gifted too, given,
learning to receive gifts

with poise my child,
I suddenly recall, time and time again,
I now hear her voice, with poise
I tell you and we smile,
you need to surrender, I say
to be given,

like I,
the words, the lines,
the lemon tree has grown
so beautifully, I wish
again I say, one day
you will be able to see

190
LIQUORICE
ALL SORTS

A little lone
cloud in the sky
drifting from the right to the
left

as day breaks
waking up to the fact that
night is over, it passed by,
travelled its full course,

waking up from out
under the darkness
light's been borne
day it's called

slowly the expanse
transforms
from black to blue
breaking on the line,
on the horizon
the colours change

and I marvel, watching
the array becoming a bouquet
of colours, brushed
feather-like light strokes, delicately
the expanse of blue joined
by a symphony of all sorts

and watching you
waiting, as if
waking up you do
the most wondrous thing

but I laugh out loud, images,
all sorts liquorice flood my mind
susceptible to double interpretation,
equivocal

it's in the waiting
in the watching
my thoughts start going
their own way, culminating,
becoming lines, growing

branches bearing fruit,
seemingly the most natural thing
watching I am,
the tree becoming strong

my laughing is what,
it does the trick

opening your eyes,
what's up you say,
knowing again
something unique
presented itself,

liquorice though
furthest from your mind
it's the morning thing
by now you know
routinely surprising

superbly the liquorice provides
morning laughter
and down the stairs I go, fetching
you your coffee
seeing as you decided too,
to shed the night

laughing as I see how
from an overturned packet
liquorice of all sorts falls
all over the place, it rains liquorice

and in my nose I get the flavour
and in my mouth the taste

peculiar to
Liquorice All Sorts

191
THE GLOW
THE AMBER THROWS

I see out
from the corner of my eye

it catches my attention into
a portion of my brain it goes

the amber of the light
through the shade of the lamp

on the stand, proudly standing
on the shelf, in the passage,

at the top, protecting
guarding the staircase

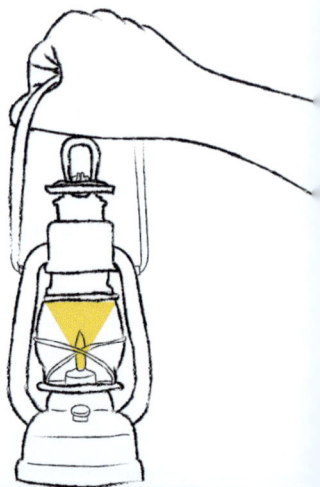

separating the levels of our
house, while all silent still

woken up I am
by the particularly loud crashing

the waves breaking on the rocks
the ocean in full language-

like in full swing
dancers-

the amber of the light
through the lamp shade rich as syrup

brown-copper mixed with gold, soft,
amber I think it's called

and with it I sense the awareness,
the beauty of amber

and it takes me far back
into the days

metal workers, melting metals,
running in richness, refining

purifying is what Word says we
will be, purified, cleaned of all

the debris removed
taken out from

out of the world
the remnant will be preserved
in Petra

and around me day breaks
less and less of the lamp amber

I see from the corner of my eye
in full view now the sun is rising

a ball of fire first,
is it my imagination, do I

see specks of amber?
then full blown in yellow

it sits in the blue
until the moon comes around

to my part of the world
reflecting its glory

just like Isra-El, that of God
the bride

all Isra-El will be saved, out of
from Petra they will go

I think while I experience
the glow the amber throws

192
THE ACUTE
STRANGENESS
OF ACCURACY

I wake up,
my head full questions
astounded I am
how can accuracy combine,
itself so well with strangeness

the acute strangeness of
the accuracy is what I find
so astounding

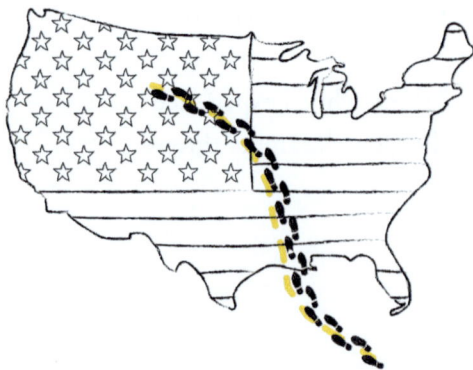

in the dream
the one I woke up with
putting me
and the hairdresser
perfectly together
where last we shared a spot
in the past

my brother too, also is there
my real brother
lending me his car,
I wake up feeling the keys
in my hand

but driving from the one
side of America to the other
as if the most natural thing,
that part I realise
my waking-up brain rejects,

waking up, our conversation
ending, making arrangements
where to leave the key
upon arrival, and off he goes

waking up, knowing suddenly
it was a dream, also knowing
the people are real, I know them
but they became dream people
that much I know, waking up

You feel my uneasiness,
questions hanging in the air
between us
aware you are I had just arrived

from somewhere else,
some place far away
visited by real people
in my dream
and my questions hang

how then this dream
of the hairdresser
that calls me flower
wherefrom does it come?

and throws into the plot, I say
my brother and his car
for a cross-country trip
right across the USA
from east to west
do we live in the USA?
never had I borrowed a car,
and on top of that, let alone, his

and as I came to my senses
the realisation of what led to the dream
presents itself with a vividness,
shocking

in the week I saw her
the hairdresser, the one
that calls me flower

in an unusual
out of character position,
confronted, challenged,
so shocked it was
hard to believe my eyes
were they not deceiving me?

my senses rejecting the fact
it was the hairdresser,
the one calling me flower,
singing praise songs
with me in church

and the understanding of how
my brain constructed the scene
into the dream, it dawned on me
my perplexity

the hairdresser in an unusual

out of character position
feeling compromised, I was
cheated, all along,
to sing praise songs in church
is the easy part, all along

and that is what
constructed the dream,
put together the scenes,
I tell you

until the next one, I say to you
I will again tell you
attempting to understand
what it is that constructs
my dreams where real people
meet me with acute accuracy
in circumstances so strange

was it real, I ask myself,
make-belief, what am I to make
borrowing a car to trek across the USA,
and the hairdresser

in the position
compromising her witness
what is it I was shown?
surely I was shown something
I say to you,

all these questions
I bombard you with
the morning still early,
daybreak not yet in full swing
and up you get to fetch
the morning tea,
leaving me be
trying to decipher my dream

I must have had it
in the minutes before a woken-up state,
able to recall
and writing it down,

in anticipation I am now awaiting night
for perhaps I have another of these,
hoping I will again,

thinking how
acutely strange is accuracy

193
LAUGHING
BY MYSELF

So dark it is
the night, pitch black
not a single thing to be seen
out- or inside

I had another one
I say to you,
as we open our eyes,
seconds apart,

the alarm screeching
meaning the power
has been out
for a while

the dark outside is
pitch black is the night
the little radio alarm's
green lights flashing,
so cute I think,

but I cannot see, the time
of night, less cute
I think, and I laugh
all by myself and about this
laughing by myself I also laugh

the time of night
remaining a mystery, up I jump
to punch the alarm pad,
wishing I can punch instead
the power company,

I can teach them a thing or two,
of power, I mumble, trying to regain my sight,
resume my night, but alas, that's
a thing of the past!

the power company cut it short, my night,
and worse, even more
right in the middle of my dream

now I sit, I'm the one sitting
with a story without an ending
I was visited again by people
no relation of each other
they were, but together they appear,
the aunt and the boy,
so funny, paintings in the bath

as I say, the plug was pulled
on my story,
now without an ending it hangs
the curtain is halfway up
or is it halfway down,
all due to power being cut, snap,
just like that we move
from light to no light

the purpose of the visit
from the aunt, the boy
with the paintings unbeknown,
my questions now remain unanswered,
and all I can do
is laugh by myself, grateful

I can still see
the funny side of things

and out of the black in our room
jumps up the image
of the photographer,
do you recall the photographer,
I say, and at this you also laugh,

together we enjoy
another moment so rare,
seeing the funny side of things,
us punching in the air
the power company

194
SUN-KISSED
CLOUDS

is what I see, I say to you
do you know

what sun-kissed clouds look like
you need to look now,

I say, to see sun-kissed clouds
candy floss, I say is no match

not a patch on the beauty
of the reddish, no pinkish sun

kissing the frame of the clouds
sitting on the horizon line

between sea and sky
they occupy space,

forming a bank
flat underneath,

beautiful free shapes
on the upside

you reminding me of
the down side and we enjoy

a rare moment,
laughing together

marvelling at creation
fresh and crisp every morning

grace is fresh every morning,
my friend says

I remember things
there are things I know

from long ago, in my memory
they have been there, always,

I say I just knew it, I've always been,
you too, I say,

do you recall when we met,
how I said, I knew you,
your soul is what's been familiar to me,
no unknown factor,

to be chosen is to be known,
God decides whom He calls,

whom He sends and when then
He takes them back, home,

into the heavenlies again
to dwell with Him

all this I tell you as the sun rises
into the beautiful blue sky,

the bank of clouds still sitting
adorning the sky with

beauty, grandeur in full display
I lose track of time, completely

watching
the sun-kissed clouds

just sitting still
in the sky, we are

195
THE
HIGH JUMP

I tell you, I will be ready for when
your return will be a glad affair
joyous the occasion
buoyant, elated, completely
out from under my skin,
I will jump high as the sky

you have not yet seen such high jump,
as high as the sky,
higher into space where
we will again be,
as before the time of separation
absence, abstinence, loneliness

apart from the other we have
been, life carried on,
losses were suffered,
some gains, here and there
isolated so sporadic,
through the valleys,
the shadows of death we moved

but up from under
we again come, surfaced
through the shadow lands,
such a lovely story that,
I tell you, do you recall, you do, you say and

receiving your coffee, the umpteenth one,
that does not matter though,
I don't care
to carry
you your coffees
as many as you want
is good by me

cup in one hand, the other busy too,
you sit, watching the stars
and low and behold there one
does it, the high jump,

the loop
you call me to see, alas I am
slow,
too much so, to see
the high jump, but even so
we laugh, thinking I am again

happiness is such a rare thing
I leave you be, time you need
to unwind, at your own pace,
we each have it, our own pace,
and with this I give
you your space

while I retreat,
into the background I go
to play with my words,
jumping high took its toll
the other stars surprised
at just how high,
calling it
the high jump

196
REACHING
CONCLUSIONS

That is what I say to you
I will have to think about
but quite unnecessary so
as you can see
I've not reached a conclusion,

the verdict, the jury still being
out- out of reach as well
if you ask me,
hoping it does not hang-

in my mind's eye I see him again,
hanging on the finest fish line,
swinging happily,
the clown at Marthie's during Easter,
and I smile

a conclusion something
to be reached, the loop closed
and open loops both of us,
we don't like,
and laugh about this jointly
in acknowledgement
agreement sugar sweet

silently realising
reaching conclusions
no simple matter,
not simply a matter of reaching

matters never are simple
in terms of conclusions

reaching seems similar
to climbing Everest, steep
the conclusion, the peak
staying out of reach,
no matter how sustained
the climbing continues

reminding me of mountains
wherefrom fountains
living waters flow,
wondering I am out loud, I say,
letting it hang, while we continue

sharing another of those
unique eastern winter afternoons
the sun soft
through our windows

I see specks, dust delicately
dangling rays gold
a fresh pot of coffee
completes the scene

having grinded the beans
myself, the aroma mingles,
becoming one with dusk descending,

taking me closer
to the conclusion,
I must give it consideration, the matter
It's always like that, I say
to you who reads the paper

savouring your coffee,
how may that be,
you ask, knowing me inside out,
space is all I need

the conclusion reaches itself
kind of funny, don't you think, how this works,

how it works for you,
you mean, you say,
making me smile at the recognition

I'm almost sure you can see
the reaching going on inside me,
I always knew you know me better than I do
myself,

never before had I known
someone like you
allowing me
reaching conclusions
in my own time

in time to come,
we will again be like that

197
THE GIFT

I woke up, understanding
the Holy Spirit comes with gifts
when He visits, the
Ruach Hako'desh,
He brings gifts

and say I to myself
while looking into the black of night-

having in this instance
to say to self,
you're not up yet,
naturally so, it being
not yet even daybreak-

why is it I never understood
the simple meaning of the word gift

knowing full well it is
the same as
I do on occasion,
I take something, a
gift

and the parallel, so striking,
it has me standing in awe at
the revelation
the alabaster broken,
out flows the oil
poured out,
priceless the value

why then will it not the same,

He came,
He brought with Him a
gift,
He went,
He left the
gift,
it remains, stays behind,
the gift,

I realise the word,
not to be mistaken
or understood outside
the plain and simple,
obvious and widely-used meaning,
simply saying
what it says,
gift

albeit unique in type,
having to acknowledge
sovereignly He decides
who to give it to,
not to be counselled too,
Him being the Councillor

and the manger scene,
the image positions itself
vividly I see
gifts brought by wise men,
the occasion, the birth
of certainly the greatest
Gift,

They gave to celebrate
He came to sacrifice
and through the ages

He looked forward, and saw me,
knowing in advance
I have to still come
have my chance on Earth

and He knew
as far back as then
which would be the gift
He would bring, and when
and then

on the appointed day He came
bringing the gift, and left it
the words to make lines
left behind the mark
of His visit

now already reaching the
second centenary,
two times hundred full,
two hundred baskets

full lemons
from the pip that fell
died in the ground
and became the lemon tree

and as the dome starts
putting its shimmer on display,
soft gold-orange,
pink brushed in between
camouflaging the blue, you stir

watching me, noticing
I'm busy harvesting, reaping,
filling the basket,
simply picking, into my hands they go

and up I look, noticing
the breeze swung,
increased its intensity, and I know
I still have to learn how to read the wind,

to determine its speed,
knowing full well it goes
where it wills,
only its effect is to be seen,

so He is too, the Spirit,
Messiah said,
and now I know that also
I now believe,
as I sit with it in my hands,
the effect of the visit, the
gift

198
MY PLAIN
PRAYER
(FOR MARIANA)

Let me run
to speak with my God
I think, as I open my eyes
only for God I have
understanding came

as I woke up swinging my short legs from bed
like the gymnast He made me to be,
rushing to get my morning tea,

to come back for my morning conversation
with the Highest, the Almighty, my Father
who has His home in heaven,
His throne room,

His feet on the earth,
where I live, all under control
called His Sovereign Divine,
and safe and secure I know
I am, because of that, blessed,

I am a sheep,
He will direct me to His right after having partaken
in the first resurrection, following Him-

watching the tribulation saints,
joining those of the first age as well,
faith like the heroes described for me
by the author of Hebrews-
the First Fruit Messiah,

so this is my plain prayer,
to thank Him for understanding,
seeing this life is not where
my happiness is found,
neither does it offer any treasures of note,

no accolades I am interested in
only in collecting little pieces
fish and bread
from the Master
through His beautiful hands
distributing grace He is
every morning fresh,
my friend regularly reminds me

and I cannot but for falling down
face to the ground
for all the mercy,
grace I have been bestowed

adoration, my praises
offering it upwards the incense
to Him my plain prayer,
in the morning, still black
the darkness much of my
surrounding reality,

agreeing with David, I am,
do not let your Spirit, my Adonai,
take His precious presence from me,
my Councillor
that will reign in the millennium
the government will be
on His mighty shoulder,

and to me

for me in my simple state
You gave the seed
that became a tree,
strong the branches
my own demonstration
of the Kingdom,
little seed, big tree

faith is what You want
in the Word
and reflecting I feel a bit
like Thomas, who had to feel and see,
his own eyes,

blessed Messiah said to the twelve, are those,
who are not in need
of seeing, just by believing,
the baskets will become filled

and praise and adoration
flow through me like a river
but from down to up,
because that's where from He is calling
arousing in me
my plain prayer

and I think, what a lovely name
is Mariana, it has a ring to it
just like Madeleine

I say to her, my friend,
let Him do the measuring,
the places will be pleasant,
just keep on believing until day
one thousand
three hundred and
thirty-five

this is
my plain prayer
to let us keep on believing

199
THE HOLE
IN THE CLOUDS

There, I say, is a hole in the clouds,
you barely move,
not convinced you heard right

right there I say, and point to the hole in the clouds
there where the thick grey mass
shows a perfectly round hole

the blue that shines through
not your everyday kind of blue
having a kind of dark steel quality to it,

and I wonder just exactly how deep
the hole is that sits roundly
in the clouds and if that steel blue sits just above
the thick grey mass of clouds

I cannot get you to be interested
far too early it is for you
especially given the morning being so greyish
giving the impression
the day will make a cold start

so the warmth of the feather mattress topper
a far more attractive option,
as if I'd asked you to choose,
imagine, I say to myself in silence, and smile

you seem to notice this,
knowing it means something,
you see the mischief, and I laugh out loud,
knowing how attractive the offer
of the feather mattress topper can be

never before we had
this wonderful mattress topper
would I have thought the bed can be so alluring

especially seen from the perspective
I can sit and look east through our windows
and be there where in the east
day breaks every single morning

I cannot wait to wake up and see
day breaking in the east,
except on days like today
where thickly the grey mass of clouds
obscures my vantage point

but the hole in the clouds
showing the steel like blue
quite impressively-looking-like-a-pool
of ice cold water

resembling what I recall
a hole in the ice looks like,
rivers iced up,
skaters taking extra care
to avoid, else leg breaking is their future

now the scene upped a notch,
hilariously funny it's become seeing I do,
the skaters side stepping these holes
in the snow, or rather ice,

same thing you say,
and I got a slight fright because
off I went on my own, skating
forgetting you exist and I must
have been talking to myself
out loud, narrating
the entire scene, monologuing

and to think this whole story
started with a
hole in the clouds,
life is funny I say to you,
disappearing somewhere between
the duvet and the feather mattress topper,

not at all interested in skaters
stepping into holes in the ice
as beautiful
and fascinating as
the hole in the clouds may be,
it's just that, a
hole in the clouds
and you laugh
I laugh too, knowing better

the hole in the clouds
is not just that, a
hole in the clouds
it's another of those powerful
demonstrations of my Adonai

it's time, I say,
to change your lens, to
adjust your angle, the
hole in the clouds is a matter
of perspective

200
SO DELICATELY
UNIQUE

are the two of us
realising that much
holding it tightly
in our fallible hands
the precious gift that's us

so delicately unique

the recognition, coming with
acknowledging, having passed by
various stations, the train,
of realising through tunnels
of vision,

tunnel vision, but we don't mind
if it's called that, we know better,
we apply it, the zoom, the focus
continually we adjust the lens

seeing only us in the reflections
of the flames, dancing against the wall,
longfellows, dreamworld people,
spider flowers and
snowmen in summer

so delicately unique
we believe in make believe
softening the reality,
the edges for each other, being

so delicately unique

we have our goal
in mind and
we have our path laid out
stone by stone we step on

we have a Father who knows
the plans He has for us,
we follow, He leads, the Conductor,
the baton in His hands indicating the beat

so delicately unique

balance is always, it's like that
so delicately unique
in the balance it hangs, is it described,
it can tip either way

I look up and point you
in the direction of the
particularly bright star
all by itself it sits
so delicately unique

I remind you it all depends
on your focus how much you see,
the star or the vast blackness of the midnight sky
being the surround
so delicately uniquely

and you take my hand in the one
and my guitar in the other and
you walk with me, home after the show,
where I partook
in the orchestra, the finest instruments in a rhythm
so delicately unique

and as we walk
I pull from my bag
my light blue checkered hat
and you look to me
in spite of it being dark,

I see
your remarkable blue-green
grey eyes, because I know that's their colour,
our souls one
so delicately unique

no substitute there will ever be
for you, and as I now
continue on my own, I still talk to you
all the time, into the long dark hours far
into the night

because I see far into the future
He gave me the ability to

so delicately, uniquely so

the finest vision
seeing beyond
the here and now
it's true

you just have to believe
you will see
through the eyes of faith

the delicacy, the uniqueness
and you will hold on to it
tightly in spite of your
hands being fallible

201
YOU PITCHED
YOUR TENT

in my heart your tent now sits
like a real Indiana Jones
reality is I really don't even
actually know Indiana Jones
never was I one
for those kinds of stories

but I think I remember a tent

perhaps my memory fails me completely
and hopelessly I go
laughing myself to pieces
for the expression on your face
tells me it's the case

fragments of joy drift between us

along the lines of the stories I tell,

you the adorable recipient
seeing without fail what I mean

not minding if I have the cat by the tail,

as long as I don't swing too viciously
violating Indiana
too much out of perspective

that's why you managed to pitch
your tent in my heart,
camping out, to your desire
you make us a fire

It's Friday night after all
that's what Indianas like us do
we make fires,
we don't care about the Joneses
keeping up does not interest us,
we have our own style

I dreamt of you last night
how you, measuring it out
washing your hands,
the outside tap sitting at the corner
of our house, so conveniently placed
we both appreciate

wanting to put a deck
at the back, your sweetly silent-
almost shy- demeanour
clearly prominent in my dream

you just go about
doing your thing, and
the tent grows bigger
and bigger

as the saying goes,
I tell you this and we laugh,
both for our own reasons,
unbeknown to each,
but for sure I know partly
you must have recalled the incident too,
sayings don't go!

you see, I say, that's why I say
you pitched your tent
in my heart, a real Indiana
you are no keeper up,
just going about,
doing your own thing
pitching your tent
in my heart

and I caught this one, the dream,
I am a dream catcher
after all is said and done,
on paper I have it now, the story,
it has legs of its own, it will run

slowly I raise, realising another of those
beautifully made-by-God days
is breaking in the east
and in my spot I am to see
and praise to God I give in return
for the fish and bread, baskets-full

and laughing, I have my own
Indiana Jones,
he lives in the tent
pitched in my heart

202
GRACE

What is it you write down,
you ask and I smile,
you evoke that in me,
constantly, a smile

it must be you being kind
a gentle soul
it's called, that's you

and it sets the scene
for the words
growing, maturing into lines

into branches, strong
bearing the fruit, many lemons
sufficient for your needs

no, not only sufficient
abundantly so, the seed
overflowing the rivers are, living

growing can be painful
pruning even more so
inseparable the two
like two sides of a coin
it comes with both, same thing
like twins, one but two

you decide to get up
make and bring the tea
you know I appreciate

we value each other
that is settled knowledge
a long time ago

so long
I cannot even remember
from when it started

bringing with it clarity
security, steadfast it is
my shield against the storm

a kind of protection beyond
human comprehension
falling short,

forcefully but breath-like
gently ever-present
all encompassing, surrounding

so I can sing,
I have a name
grafted-in gentile

is my name, yours too,
if you believe,
put your trust in Him

lean into Him,
with all you have
without fail He protects,

He shields, the arrows
can come powerless, they are
and I know that settles it for me

case closed, conclusion drawn
Everest reached,
the climb complete

ascended I have
to the pinnacle, the higher
plane
my homeland

and in front of me you stand
tea in hand, in all this time
the words matured into lines
you were making
and brought, the tea
evoking in me a smile

appreciation the canal
through which it flows
the grace

203
STRATA

I am privileged
no, not privileged, I say,
that now sounding understatement-like,
it has a different ring to it

blessed is more like it

Messiah says blessed are those
He spells it out
the character traits
of those who are
in the sermon on the mount

many heard,
some listened,
others heeded,
some followed,
twelve were chosen, elected

making me think of strata

reaching in my mind
quite a different place,
you bringing me back, saying
you were going to tell me about,

and neither of us
can remember,
our thoughts drifting
It is Saturday after all
we allow ourselves to drift

in and out
the one to the other
layers
strata forming,
taking shape
in my brain

and we again laugh,
goodness merging
with winter sun,
becoming one
drifting between us
are then sun then joy

delicate fragments of
associations so strong,

I realise afresh,
produce from the market,
our small-town,
a village it's called,
we like it like that,
small, quaint, quiet,
slow-paced in time too
standing still, talking to
people walking on the way

and all this time,
the entire Saturday,
strata
is what's living in my mind
my thoughts revolve around
blessed are those

counting myself blessed
I know what being protected
feels like, having witnessed it,
seen it, experienced it
first hand as well

the blessedness
of being protected

as if snatched, held on to
pulled from the fire unscathed
like Daniel's friends
no trace of smoke
on the clothes still white,
clean as from before

and still the idea of strata
lingers, it made its nest in my
mind filled with strata
and an understanding
of being blessed

204
CLARITY
OF THOUGHT

I woke up
from sleeping deep
in my surrounds
I don't hear a thing,
nothing but
sporadically, here and there
some morning sounds,

crystal clear
through the air
as if thin

Realising I need
clarity of thought
in a generation misled
on a scale so global,
it's a beast and all follow,
masses, all and sundry

without thinking through
the logic which I cannot see

having to stand strong
with the clarity of thought
my only protection,
the mind of Christ
lived in by Ruach Hako'desh

going against the grain
of the times,
swimming against the tide

on uniquely different a path
such as the twelve, chosen
paying prices, each their own,
suffering for having
clarity of thought

the Light the Messiah brought,
the field with the treasure,
found a knowing so certain
the conviction
a clarity of thought
undeniably so, the joy

the ability to discern
where my real safety lies

the people who live in darkness saw a big light
Me too, I saw the light

and I realise with
clarity of thought
what a really long story
I've become part of,
I must serve Messiah from the place
measured out for me,
simply because it's a beautiful place
called

clarity of thought

205
REMARKABLY
RECEPTIVE

Delicate fragments
of joy and sun
hanging
in the air, the space
between us happy
the surrounds crowning us

your receptivity remarkable

blessed, having eternal life
hearing to whom belongs the Kingdom
says Messiah

and I wake up thinking
how double-edged His words are,
required to be listened to
with discernment, to grasp
the full meaning, catch it all
in its fullness

indeed an attribute of the Word
described by the writer
to the Hebrews, and

I see them
huddled around
on the mount
establishing in their hearts
and minds His Kingdom

quite another kind
having to reprogramme
their style, the modus operandi,
getting a sense of what's required to repent

to change your mind,
turn around
in another direction
away from the former way
walking in the Way

from here on
Seek first the Kingdom
is His command,
to inherit the earth

and as I look up
I see you in the sun
and the joy hangs
in the air, in the space
between us floating are
little finite specks so sweet

and I think again
how remarkable is
your receptivity

206
THE JUBILEE
ARRIVED

So sweet this little lamp,
wishing I am you could too share in the
delight
the little lamp provided me with
tonight
a Chinese lamp if I understood
right,
special, too cute

It went out
for no reason

I could not get it on again,
no matter how hard I tried,
and as I was sitting now

turning around
for no reason

I saw to my surprise
it went on
for no reason

and I think God our Father
in His Divine Sovereign grace
wanted me to see the light
He is able to provide,
I just need to look onto Him
for powerful deeds

Indeed He provides
the light
that overcomes the darkness

and in my heart raised a song
of praise, it bursts,
only one desire I have,
to sing,
the jubilee

He will not forsake nor leave me
for no reason,
small or big
out of His hands
I will not be snatched!

for no reason,
none at all

just walk I should
in His light
His Kingdom all I seek

He will provide
all and more
than what I need

Again He confirmed
His presence to me,

for no reason,
none other than

wanting me to know
He is Father, I, child

using the little lamp so cute
Chinese I believe

Let there be light,
Word said
and there was light
so true the Word

for no reason
other than
for me
just to believe
He is the Light
powerfully He demonstrates

for no reason necessary
other than just
for me to believe

seeking I should firstly
His Kingdom, He will give
all else I need to see
down the ages into eternity,

adjust your lens, I say to you,

lazy we've become, laid back
you with the paper,
us stretching out in the balmy
sun of the eastern winter afternoon,
rays of joy in the space,
the air between us sweetness

time for our walk to the beach
to listen to the sails
whisp whisp they make
soft evening lights coming on
in the cafés filling with
weekend guests

I respond to your
outstretched hand,
pulling me up in one motion
putting on my head
my light blue checkered hat,

I grab my guitar to write
a new song,
one of praise
for the jubilee,
it has arrived

207
NIGHT IS APPROACHING
(FOR STEPHEN)

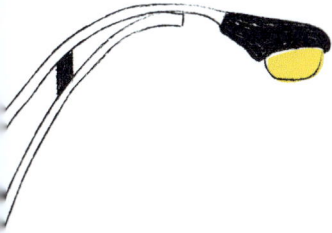

Just come on they have,
the street lights like little
beacons of hope, a bit early
in my opinion, I say to you
for what it's worth

knowing you will laugh at me
but not in a funny way,
more like laughing in agreement
a knowing so unique

my opinion going astray, far off
carried over the bay
from where we find our silence
in the surround
stretching itself out
over the ocean like a tent covering,
providing for

acute silence, just what we need
realising that much standing on the balcony
evaluating the time of arrival
of the beacons of hope as
night is approaching
as if commanded,

signalling
evening moving in on us
from the horizon
are the pinkish white seashell pearl clouds,
cotton wool travelling in time

willing we are to believe,
hanging on to the beacon of hope alive in our hearts,
safely stowed away,

the Rock on which we built
our house, not on sand,
being we are,
able to wither the storm,
fear an unknown factor, absent

and we watch them as
across they go, slow
in their own time and,
we count our blessings
for having a balcony

from where we can become
one with each other and
night that is approaching
taking it easy
slowly we move into
night that's approaching,
carried along by evening the passage way,
the carrier of
the approaching night

and we
get carried away too
by the salty sea air
we arrived home with
night that's approaching

with the realisation so stark
our values so uniquely its own
in sync, our rhythm so different,
just alone with each other
we want to be as
night is approaching

having eyes only for eternity
the journey the pursuit
not to accumulate wealth
the words, the tree growing
on route to Everest,
the higher plane,

the Mount of Olives
is where He will plant His throne